Math Essentials

Chad Troutwine · Markus Moberg · Brian Galvin · Mark Glenn · Cliff Smith

Co-Founders	Chad Troutwine
	Markus Moberg
Managing Editor	Mark Glenn
Director of Academic Programs	Brian Galvin
Interior Design	Miriam Lubow
	Lisa Johnson
Cover Design	Nick Mason
	Mike Miller
Contributing Editors	David Newland
	Neil Moakley
	Jason Sun
	Jeff Lev
Contributing Writer	Nick Strauss

A successful educational program is only as good as the people who teach it, and Veritas Prep is fortunate to have many of the world's finest GMAT instructors on its team.

Not only does that team know how to teach a strong curriculum, but it also knows how to help create one. This lesson book would not be possible without the hundreds of suggestions we have received from our talented faculty all across the world—from Seattle, Detroit, and Miami to London, Singapore, and Dubai. Their passion for excellence helped give birth to a new curriculum that is far better than what we could have created on our own.

Our students also deserve a very special thanks. Thousands of them have provided us with something priceless: enthusiastic feedback that has guided us in creating the most comprehensive GMAT preparation course available on the market today.

We therefore dedicate this revised lesson book to all Veritas Prep instructors and students who have tackled the GMAT and given us their valuable input along the way.

Table of Contents

Lesson 0 Introduction

This lesson provides in-depth coverage of the mathematical fundamentals you will see on the GMAT. Veritas Prep has performed extensive research on the test – nothing presented here is extraneous. In fact, everything here is essential to a strong performance on the GMAT. Once you have these fundamentals down, you'll be able to fully utilize the Veritas Prep strategies found in the upcoming Quant lessons. To maximize the value of your time, you should begin with the Math Essentials pretest to determine which sections to study.

Math Essentials Diagnostic Test

You may use a notepad, but do not use a calculator when solving the problems below. Although you may guess on the GMAT, the purpose of this test is to determine any areas where you need some additional work. Therefore, do not guess; if you do not know how to solve the problem, leave the answer blank.

1. Which of the following is a real number?

(A) $\pi\ (= 3.1415926\ldots)$

(B) 13

(C) $\sqrt{2}\ (= 1.414141\ldots)$

(D) All of the above

(E) None of the above

2. Which of the following is an integer?

(A) -17

(B) 0

(C) 23

(D) All of the above

(E) None of the above

3.   Which of the following is a factor of 56?

(A)   1

(B)   4

(C)   7

(D)   All of the above

(E)   None of the above

4.   Which of the following is a multiple of 6?

(A)   -18

(B)   0

(C)   36

(D)   All of the above

(E)   None of the above

5.   If 43 is divided by 13, what is the remainder?

(A)   3

(B)   4

(C)   5

(D)   6

(E)   None of the above

6. When two-digit integer q is divided by 9, the remainder is 4. If q is a multiple of 7, which of the following could be the units digit of q?

(A) 0

(B) 1

(C) 5

(D) 7

(E) 9

7. When integer i is divided by 3, the remainder is 1. When i is divided by 4, the remainder is 3. If i is greater than 5 but less than 30, what is its value?

(A) 13

(B) 15

(C) 16

(D) 19

(E) 23

8. Both n and m are integers. When n is divided by m, the remainder is 3. If m is divisible by 4 and n is less than 20, which of the following could be the value of n?

(A) 10

(B) 11

(C) 13

(D) 17

(E) None of the above

9. What is the fraction $\frac{5}{8}$ expressed as a decimal (rounded to the nearest hundredth)?

(A) 0.45

(B) 0.50

(C) 0.58

(D) 0.63

(E) 0.68

10. $\left(\frac{200,000}{0.05}\right) \cdot \frac{1}{100}$ equals what?

(A) 400

(B) 4,000

(C) 40,000

(D) 400,000

(E) 4,000,000

11. What is the value of the product $(\frac{375}{16}) \cdot (\frac{64}{25})$?

(A) 15

(B) 60

(C) 92

(D) 60%

(E) None of the above

12.   A bacterial population doubles every two hours. If the initial population is
        100,000 cells, how many cells will there be 8 hours later?

(A)   160,000

(B)   320,000

(C)   800,000

(D)   1,600,000

(E)   25,600,000

13.   To what can the fraction $\frac{25}{275}$ be reduced?

(A) $\frac{1}{11}$

(B) $\frac{1}{12}$

(C) $\frac{1}{13}$

(D) $\frac{1}{15}$

(E) $\frac{25}{275}$

14.   To what can the fraction $\frac{66}{275}$ be reduced?

(A) $\frac{2}{5}$

(B) $\frac{3}{25}$

(C) $\frac{6}{25}$

(D) $\frac{66}{275}$

(E)   Other

15. What is the product of $\frac{3}{7}$ and $\frac{49}{15}$?

(A) $\frac{5}{7}$

(B) $\frac{45}{49}$

(C) $\frac{49}{45}$

(D) $\frac{7}{5}$

(E)   Other

16. What number divided by $\frac{13}{19}$ equals $\frac{133}{65}$?

(A) $\frac{5}{7}$

(B) $\frac{5}{19}$

(C) $\frac{7}{5}$

(D) $\frac{19}{7}$

(E)   Other

17. What is 35% of 700?

(A)   200

(B)   245

(C)   2,000

(D)   2,450

(E)   Other

18.   What is the percentage change if a number is increased from 140 to 175?

(A)   20%

(B)   25%

(C)   30%

(D)   35%

(E)   Other

19.   If a fund that has an initial value of $1,300,000 goes down by 15%, what is the final value of the fund?

(A) $195,000

(B) $1,005,000

(C) $1,105,000

(D) $1,195,000

(E)   Other

20.   If a stock decreases in value from $87.50 to $62.50, what is the percent change?

(A)   - 20%

(B)   - 25%

(C)   - 29%

(D)   - 38%

(E)   - 43%

21. The insurance expense in 2004 for a certain business was $160,000. If this expense was 33% more than in 2003, what was the insurance expense in 2003?

(A) $53,333

(B) $106,667

(C) $120,000

(D) $173,333

(E)   Other

22. If $\frac{5}{12}$ of 360 is increased by 200%, what is the result?

(A)   300

(B)   450

(C)   720

(D)   1,728

(E)   2,592

23. What percent of 625 is 300?

(A)   21%

(B)   48%

(C)   52%

(D)   208%

(E)   Other

24.   Baxter is mixing a concentrated pigment with a solvent in the ratio of 2:9.
       If he has $3\frac{3}{4}$ gallons of the pigment, how many gallon cans of solvent will he
       need to use up all the pigment?

(A)   9

(B)   15

(C)   17

(D)   34

(E)   Other

25.   An alloy contains only lead, copper, and tin in the ratio 2:3:1. How many pounds
       of lead are there in 54 pounds of the alloy?

(A)   9

(B)   18

(C)   27

(D)   36

(E)   Other

26. $\frac{3^9}{3^6}$ equals what?

(A) $\frac{1}{9}$

(B)   9

(C)   27

(D)   81

(E)   Other

27. $\dfrac{15x^3y^5}{3xy}$ equals what?

(A) $5x^2y^4$

(B) $12x^2y^4$

(C) $5x^4y^6$

(D) $12x^4y^6$

(E)   Other

28. $\dfrac{16x^6}{4x^{-4}}$ equals what?

(A) $4x^2$

(B) $4x^{10}$

(C) $12x^2$

(D) $12x^{10}$

(E)   Other

29. $(3x^2)^3$ equals what?

(A) $3x^5$

(B) $3x^6$

(C) $9x^5$

(D) $9x^6$

(E) $27x^6$

30.   What is the product of $4\sqrt{6}\sqrt{24}$?

(A) $4\sqrt{30}$

(B)   12

(C)   48

(D)   144

(E)   Other

31.   Eliminate the denominator of $\frac{\sqrt{3} - 9}{\sqrt{3}}$.

(A) $1 - 3\sqrt{3}$

(B) $3 - 3\sqrt{3}$

(C) $3 - 9\sqrt{3}$

(D) -6

(E)   Other

32.   What is the sum of $3\sqrt{2} + 3\sqrt{2} + 3\sqrt{98}$?

(A) $3\sqrt{102}$

(B) $9\sqrt{2}$

(C) $21\sqrt{2}$

(D) $27\sqrt{2}$

(E) $3\sqrt{396}$

33.   If $6(2x + 3) = 4x + 74$, what is the value of x?

(A)   7

(B)   8

(C)   9

(D)   10

(E)   Other

34.   If $x + 2y = 8$ and $x - y = 2$, where do the lines intersect (expressed as x,y)?

(A)   (2,4)

(B)   (2,8)

(C)   (4,2)

(D)   (8,2)

(E)   Other

35.   If $x - 2 \leq z \leq x + 5$, where does the value of x lie in terms of z?

(A) $z - 5 \leq x \leq z$

(B) $z - 5 \leq x \leq z + 2$

(C) $z - 2 \leq x \leq z + 5$

(D) $z - 2 \leq x \leq z$

(E)   Other

36. A tank contains 500 kg of a solution that is 4 percent potassium chloride by weight. If 100 kg of water evaporates from the tank, the remaining solution will be approximately what percent potassium chloride?

(A) 2%

(B) 2.5%

(C) 5%

(D) 17%

(E) 20%

37. Of the 2,000 employees who work at company ABC, 80% are factory workers. If the number of factory workers will be reduced by ¼, what percent of the total number of remaining employees would then be factory workers?

(A) 25%

(B) 60%

(C) 75%

(D) 80%

(E) Other

38. Two years ago, Raj was twice as old as Poonam was then. Six years ago, Raj was three times as old as Poonam was then. How old is Raj?

(A) 10

(B) 12

(C) 18

(D) 21

(E) 24

39.   Pipe A can fill a tank in 2 days. Pipe B can fill the same tank in 4 days. If the tank starts empty and the two pipes each run for 8 hours, how full will the tank be?

(A) $\frac{1}{24}$ full

(B) $\frac{1}{8}$ full

(C) $\frac{1}{4}$ full

(D) $\frac{1}{3}$ full

(E) $\frac{3}{4}$ full

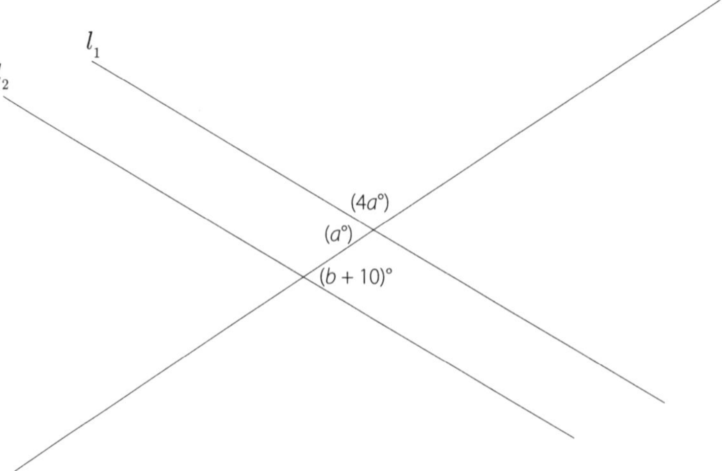

l_1 and l_2 are parallel.

40.   In the figure above, the value of b is which of the following?

(A)   20

(B)   26

(C)   30

(D)   36

(E)   42

41. A triangle has an area of x and a height of y. What is the length of the base perpendicular to that height?

(A) $\dfrac{x}{y}$

(B) $\dfrac{y}{x}$

(C) $\dfrac{2x}{y}$

(D) $\dfrac{2y}{x}$

(E) $\dfrac{y2}{x}$

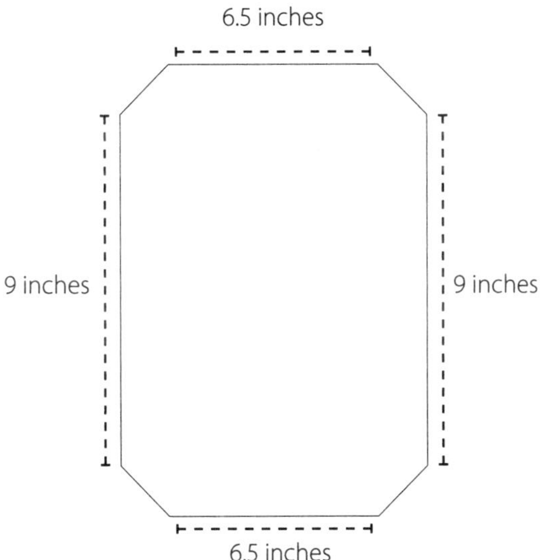

42. A rectangular piece of paper measuring 8½ by 11 inches has four identical triangles clipped off from its corners, a shown above. What is the area in square inches of the remaining piece of paper?

(A) 86½

(B) 88

(C) 89½

(D) 91½

(E) 93½

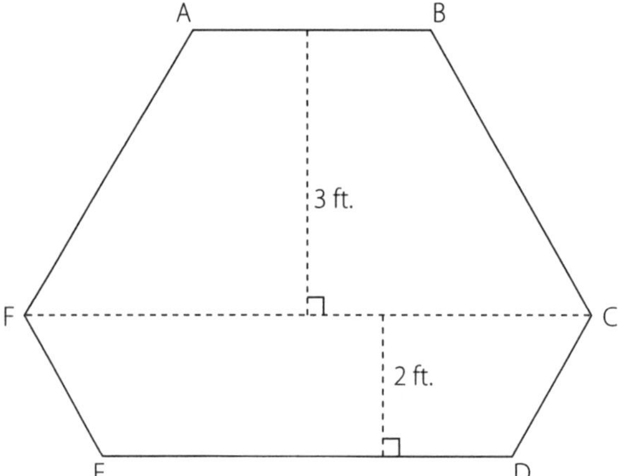

43.   Flowerbed ABCDEF is in the shape shown above, where AB, CF, and DE are all parallel. If AB = 1 ft., CF = 5 ft., and DE = 4 ft., what is the area of the flowerbed in square ft.?

(A)   16

(B)   18

(C)   19

(D)   20

(E)   22

44.   If the radius of Circle A is twice the diameter of Circle B, then how many times the area of Circle B is the area of Circle A?

(A)   2

(B)   4

(C)   8

(D)   16

(E)   32

45.   The circumference of a circle is 10. What is its radius?

(A) $\frac{10}{\pi}$

(B) $\frac{5}{\pi}$

(C) 5π

(D) 10π

(E) 20π

46.   The square in the figure above has a side of 5. A circle is perfectly inscribed in the square. What is the area of the shaded region?

(A) $25(1 - \frac{\pi}{4})$

(B) $5(1 - \frac{\pi}{4})$

(C) $25 - \frac{5\pi}{4}$

(D) $5 - \frac{25\pi}{4}$

(E) $5 + \frac{5\pi}{4}$

47.   Which of the following equations forms the line with the greatest slope?

(A) $y = -6x + 3$

(B) $y = 6x - 3$

(C) $4y = 28x - 12$

(D) $x + y = 46$

(E) $\dfrac{(y + 4)}{(x - 3)} = 13$

48. What is the x-intercept of the line described by $2y = 4x + 5$?

(A)   -5

(B)   -4

(C) $\dfrac{-5}{4}$

(D)   4

(E)   5

Answers

1. **(D)**
Imaginary numbers (the square roots of negative numbers) are the only numbers which are NOT real numbers. Irrational numbers (such as π and the square root of 2) have an infinite number of decimal places, but ARE real numbers. The correct answer is (D).

2. **(D)**
Integers are whole numbers, whether positive, negative, or zero. The correct answer is (D).

3. **(D)**
When the number 56 is divided by 1, 4, or 7, the quotient is an integer, so all three are factors of 56. The correct answer is (D).

4. **(D)**
A multiple is the product of a number (in this case 6) and ANY integer, positive, negative, or zero. Therefore -18 (6 · 3), 0 (6 · 0), and 36 (6 · 6) are all multiples of 6 and the correct answer is (D).

5. **(B)**
$43 = 3 \cdot 13$ (which is 39) + 4. The remainder is 4, answer (B).

6. **(E)**
The integer q is a multiple of 7, and when divided by 9 has a remainder of 4. Based on the remainder when dividing by 9, we can say that $q = 9n + 4$ (where n is an integer). A table can help us determine which numbers satisfy both conditions.

Multiples of 9 ($9n$)	$9n + 4$	Multiples of 7
9	13	14
18	22	28
27	31	35
36	40	42
45	49	49

The correct answer is (E).

7. **(D)**

When the integer *i* is divided by 3, the remainder is 1, so we can say that $i = 3k + 1$. When *i* is divided by 4, the remainder is 3, so we can say that $i = 4m + 3$. Again, a table can help determine which number satisfies both conditions.

3k	3k + 1	4m + 3	4m
6	7	7	4
9	10	11	8
12	13	15	12
15	16	19	16
18	19	23	20
21	22		

The correct answer is (D).

8. **(B)**

When *n* is divided by *m*, the remainder is 3, so $n = mp + 3$ (where *p* is an integer). Since *m* is divisible by 4, it is a multiple of 4, so we can say $m = 4q$ (where *q* is another integer), and $n = 4pq + 3$. A table shows an exploration of possible values of *n*:

p	q	4pq	4pq + 3
1	1	4	7
2	1	8	11

The correct answer is (B).

9. **(D)**

$\frac{1}{8} = 0.125; \frac{5}{8} = 0.625$. When rounding, one rounds up if the next digit (5 in this case) is between 5 and 9, so 0.625 is rounded to 0.63. The correct answer is (D).

10. **(C)**

Using scientific notation (powers of ten) simplifies this problem.

$$\frac{200,000}{0.05} \cdot \frac{1}{100} = \frac{2 \cdot 10^5}{5 \cdot 10^{-2}} \cdot \frac{1}{10^2} = 0.4 \cdot 10^5 = 40,000 \text{ (answer C)}$$

11. **(B)**

$$\frac{375}{16} \cdot \frac{64}{25} = \frac{375}{25} \cdot \frac{64}{16} = \frac{25 \cdot 15}{25} \cdot \frac{16 \cdot 4}{16} = 15 \cdot 4 = 60$$

Finding common factors can greatly simplify many calculations. The correct answer is (B).

12. **(D)**

The population doubles every 2 hours, so it doubles 4 times in 8 hours:
$2 \cdot 2 \cdot 2 \cdot 2 \cdot 100{,}000$ cells $= 16 \cdot 100{,}000$ cells $= 1{,}600{,}000$ cells (answer D).

13. **(A)**

To reduce $\frac{25}{275}$, think of how many quarters there are in each number: $\frac{25}{275} = \frac{1 \cdot 25}{11 \cdot 25} = \frac{1}{11}$.

14. **(C)**

To reduce the fraction, factor both numerator and denominator: $\frac{66}{275} = \frac{2 \cdot 3 \cdot 11}{5 \cdot 5 \cdot 11} = \frac{6}{25}$.

15. **(D)**

$$\frac{3}{7} \cdot \frac{49}{15} = \frac{3}{7} \cdot \frac{7 \cdot 7}{3 \cdot 5} = \frac{7}{5}$$

16. **(C)**

$$\text{So } X = \frac{133}{65} \cdot \frac{13}{19} = \frac{19 \cdot 7}{5 \cdot 13} \cdot \frac{13}{19} = \frac{7}{5}$$

17. **(B)**

$$\frac{35\%}{100\%} \cdot 700 = 35 \cdot 7 = 245$$

18. **(B)**

$$\frac{175 - 140}{140} \cdot 100\% = \frac{35}{70 \cdot 2} \cdot 100\% = \frac{35}{35 \cdot 4} \cdot 100\% = 25\%$$

19. **(C)**

The decrease is 15% of $1,300,000: 10% ($130,000) plus 5% (half 10%: $65,000)

So the final value is the initial value: $1,300,000
                    less the decrease   - 195,000
                         Final value: $1,105,000

20. **(C)**

$$\frac{\$62.50 - \$87.50}{\$87.50} \cdot 100\% = -\frac{\$25}{\$87.50} \cdot 100\% = -\frac{\frac{2}{8} \cdot \$100}{\frac{7}{8} \cdot \$100} \cdot 100\% = -29\%$$

21. **(C)**

Since the insurance expense is 33% higher, it has grown by a third.

So: $\frac{4}{3}X = \$160{,}000$ $X = \frac{3}{4} \$160{,}000 = \$120{,}000$ (answer C)

22. **(B)**

Increasing by 200% means increasing to $3x$ (300%) of the original number.

So: $\frac{5}{12} \cdot 360 \cdot 3 = \frac{5}{\cancel{12}} \cdot \cancel{12} \cdot 30 \cdot 3 = 450$ (answer B)

23. **(B)**

$\frac{300}{625} \cdot 100\% = \frac{3 \cdot 4 \cdot 25}{5 \cdot 5 \cdot 25} \cdot 100\% = \frac{12}{25} \cdot \frac{4}{4} \cdot 100\% = \frac{48}{\cancel{100}} \cdot \cancel{100}\% = 48\%$ (answer B)

24. **(C)**

$\frac{2 \text{ gal. pigment}}{9 \text{ gal. pigment}} = \frac{3\frac{3}{4} \text{ gal. pigment}}{X \text{ gal. solvent}}$ So $2X = 9 \cdot \frac{15}{4}$ and $X = \frac{135}{8} = 16\frac{7}{8}$

Since Baxter must buy gallon cans, he must buy 17 gallons (answer C).

25. **(B)**

	Lead	Copper	Tin	Total
Ratio	2	3	1	6
Weight (lbs)	18			54

Lead constitutes 2 parts of the 6 parts in total, so it is $\frac{1}{3}$ of the weight.
So in 54 lbs. of alloy, the amount of lead is $\frac{1}{3} \cdot 54$ lbs. $= 18$ lbs.

26. **(C)**

$\frac{3^9}{3^6} = 3^9 \cdot 3^{-6} = 3^{9-6} = 3^3 = 27$

27. **(A)**

$\frac{15x^3y^5}{3xy} = \frac{3 \cdot 5}{3} x^{3-1} y^{5-1} = 5x^2y^4$

28. **(B)**

$\frac{16x^6}{4x^4} = \frac{4 \cdot 4}{4} x^{6-(-4)} = 4x^{10}$

29. **(E)**
$(3x^2)^3 = 3^3\, x^{2\cdot 3} = 27x^6$

30. **(C)**
$4\sqrt{6}\sqrt{24} = 4\sqrt{(6\cdot 24)} = 4\sqrt{(144)} = 4\cdot 12 = 48$

31. **(A)**

$$\frac{\sqrt{3}-9}{\sqrt{3}}\cdot\frac{\sqrt{3}}{\sqrt{3}} = \frac{3-9\sqrt{3}}{3} = 1 - 3\sqrt{3}$$

32. **(D)**
$3\sqrt{2} + 3\sqrt{2} + 3\sqrt{98} = 6\sqrt{2} + 3\sqrt{(49\cdot 2)} = 6\sqrt{2} + (3\cdot 7)\sqrt{2} = (6 + 21)\sqrt{2} = 27\sqrt{2}$

33. **(A)**

Given:	$6(2x + 3) = 4x + 74$
Eliminate parentheses:	$12x + 18 = 4x + 74$
Subtract 4x from both sides:	$8x + 18 = 74$
Subtract 18 from both sides:	$8x = 56$
Divide both sides by 8:	$x = 7$

34. **(C)**
The lines $x + 2y = 8$ and $x - y = 2$ intersect where the values of x and y satisfy both equations, so we must solve this system of two linear equations.
Step 1: express one variable in terms of the other: $x = y + 2$
Step 2: substitute this in the other equation: $(y + 2) + 2y = 8$ $3y = 6$ $y = 2$
Step 3: solve for the other variable: $x = y + 2 = 2 + 2 = 4$
So the lines intersect where $x = 4$ and $y = 2$, the coordinate point (4,2)

35. **(B)**
$x - 2 \leq z \leq x + 5$
Manipulate the first inequality $x - 2 \leq z$ to isolate x.
Add 2 to both sides: $x \leq z + 2$
Manipulate the second inequality $z \leq x + 5$ to isolate x.
Subtract 5 from both sides: $z - 5 \leq x$
Combine the two expressions to bracket x.
$z - 5 \leq x \leq z + 2$ (answer B).

36. **(C)**

$$\frac{4\%}{100\%}\,500 \text{ kg solution} = 20 \text{ kg potassium chloride}$$

$$\frac{20 \text{ kg potassium chloride}}{500 \text{ kg} - 100 \text{ kg (evaporated)}}\cdot 100\% = \frac{20}{400}\cdot 100\% = 5\%$$

37. (C)

2000 employees $\cdot \frac{80\%}{100\%}$ factory workers = 1600 factory workers.

Number of factory workers reduced by $\frac{1}{4} : \frac{1}{4} \cdot 1600 = 400$ factory workers cut.

Number of factory workers remaining: $1600 - 400 = 1200$ factory workers

Number of employees remaining: $2000 - 400 = 1600$ employees

$\frac{1200 \text{ factory workers}}{1600 \text{ employees}} \cdot 100\% = \frac{3 \cdot 4 \cdot \cancel{100}}{4 \cdot 4 \cdot \cancel{100}} \cdot 100\% = 75\%$

38. (C)

Two years ago, Raj was twice as old as Poonam was then.

$R - 2 = 2(P-2) = 2P - 4 \qquad R = 2P - 2$

Six years ago, Raj was three times as old as Poonam was then.

$R - 6 = 3(P-6) = 3P - 18 \qquad R = 3P - 12$

Substitute R from first equation in R for second equation:

$2P - 2 = 3P - 12$

Subtract 2P from both sides of the equation:

$-2 = P - 12$

Add 12 to both sides:

$10 = P$

Substitute for P in first equation:

$R = 2(10) - 2 = 18$

39. (C)

Pipe A can fill a tank in 2 days, so $R_A = \frac{1 \text{ tank}}{2 \text{ days}}$.

Pipe B can fill the tank in 4 days, so $R_B = \frac{1 \text{ tank}}{4 \text{ days}}$.

Running together, the combined rate is:

$R_A + R_B = \frac{1 \text{ tank}}{2 \text{ days}} + \frac{1 \text{ tank}}{4 \text{ days}} = \left(\frac{2}{4} + \frac{1}{4}\right) \frac{\text{tanks}}{\text{day}} = \frac{3 \text{ tanks}}{4 \text{ days}}$

Using both pipes for 8 hours:

$8 \cancel{\text{ hrs}} \frac{1 \cancel{\text{ day}}}{24 \cancel{\text{ hrs}}} \cdot 3 \text{ tanks}/4 \cancel{\text{ days}} = \frac{1}{4} \text{ tank (answer C)}$

40. (B)

Because they form a straight line, the angles measuring a and $4a$ must sum to 180°:

$a + 4a = 180 \rightarrow 5a = 180 \rightarrow a = 36$. Because the lines are parallel, $b + 10$ must also equal 36. Thus $b = 26$.

41. (C)

Area of a triangle $= \frac{bh}{2}$. Here, $x = \frac{by}{2}$. Thus $b = \frac{2x}{y}$.

42. (D)

The easiest way to calculate the area of the remaining piece of paper is to find the area of the original piece of paper and then subtract the areas of the corners that have been clipped off. The area of the original piece of paper is 8½ ·11 = 93½ square inches. Each of the clipped triangles has a base and height of one inch each. Therefore each clipped triangle has an area of $\frac{(1 \cdot 1)}{2}$ = ½ square inch. Therefore the area of the remaining piece of paper is 93 ½ - (4 · ½) = 93½ - 2 = 91½ square inches.

43. (B)

To find the area of the flowerbed, find the areas of the two trapezoids and add them together. The area of the top trapezoid is ½ (1 + 5) · 3 = 9. The area of the bottom trapezoid is ½ (5 + 4) · 2 = 9 → 9 + 9 = 18 square ft.

44. (D)

If the radius of Circle A is twice the diameter of Circle B, then it is four times the radius of Circle B: $r_A = 2d_B = 4r_B$. The area of A is then $\pi(4r_B)^2 = 16\pi r_B^2$. The area of B is πr_B^2. Thus, the area of Circle A is 16 times the area of Circle B.

45. (B)

The circumference of a circle equals twice its radius times π: C = 10 = $2\pi r$. Thus $r = \frac{5}{\pi}$.

46. (A)

To find the area of the shaded region, find the area of the square and subtract the area of the circle. The area of the square is 5^2 = 25. If the side of the square is 5, the diameter of the circle is also 5 and its radius is $\frac{5}{2}$. The area of the circle is then $\pi(\frac{5}{2})^2 = \frac{25\pi}{4}$. The area of the square minus the area of the circle is 25 - $\frac{25\pi}{4}$. This is not one of the choices, but we can factor out a 25 to get $25(1 - \frac{\pi}{4})$.

47. (E)

To find the slope of each line, we must know what m would be if each equation were put in $y = mx + b$ form. In choice A, m = - 6. In B, m = 6. In C, we can see that by dividing both sides by 4, we will get m = 7. In D, by subtracting x from both sides we will get m = -1. In E, by multiplying both sides by $(x - 3)$ we will get m = 13. (Note that subtracting both sides by 4, which is the last step to get the equation in $y = mx + b$ form, will not affect the value of m.) Thus the equation in choice (E) has the greatest slope.

48. (C)

To find the x-intercept, set y equal to 0 and substitute:
$2(0) = 4x + 5 \rightarrow -5 = 4x \rightarrow x = \frac{-5}{4}$

Math Essentials

As you will find in the subsequent quantitative lessons, the GMAT is uniquely constructed to assess the quantitative and analytical abilities of its examinees through questions that almost exclusively feature high school level mathematics skills. While no trigonometry or calculus concepts are required, the GMAT remains a rigorous quantitative examination as it forces examinees to demonstrate thorough facility with skills in the fields of Arithmetic, Algebra, Geometry, Permutations and Combinations, Probability, Statistics, and Number Properties. Throughout the Veritas Prep program, you will learn and/or review these skills and the ways in which they will be tested.

In order to maximize the value of your study time during the course, however, it is important to recognize that all questions will require the use of arithmetic and/or algebraic fundamentals to some degree. Accordingly, you should plan to spend time before your course begins ensuring that you can comfortably apply these fundamental skills, so that you can focus more of your course time on the GMAT-specific applications of them.

This lesson is designed to help you assess your fundamental math skills, and to enable you to become comfortable and efficient with them prior to beginning the Veritas Prep course. While these topics will also be covered in the classroom, the Veritas Prep lesson materials will most often use them as building blocks toward more advanced concepts. Therefore, you should feel comfortable wiith the fundamental math skills covered in this lesson prior to beginning the course. Use this lesson to comprehensively prepare you to build upon these fundamentals.

Basic Definitions

Integers

An integer is any "whole" number, i.e. not a fraction or decimal. Positive integers are integers greater than 0. Negative integers are integers less than 0. 0 is also an integer.

Example: -47, -12, -2, -1, 0, 1, 2, 3, 8, 12, 17
The following numbers are not integers: -¼ ¾, 1.625, 3.14

Even integers:
Any integer that, when divided by 2, results in another integer.

Example: (-4, -2, -0, 2, 4, … 244, 246, 248, …)

Odd integers:
Any integer that, when divided by 2, does not result in another integer.

Example: (-5, -3, -1, 1, 3, 5, … 245, 247, 249, …)

Consecutive integers:
Any set of integers where each integer is equal to the previous integer plus 1.

Example: (-3, -2, -1, 0, 1, 2, 3, 4, 5, 6, 7, 8)

Consecutive Odd Integers:
Any set of odd integers where each integer is equal to the previous integer plus 2.

Example: (-3, -1, 1, 3, 5, 7, 9)

Consecutive Even Integers:
Any set of even integers where each integer is equal to the previous integer plus 2.

Example: (-4, -2, 0, 2, 4, 6, 8)

Divisor (or Factor)

For an integer N, a divisor is a positive integer that can divide N into another integer.

Examples
For the number 100, the following are divisors:
100, 50, 25, 20, 10, 5, 4, 2, 1

*The following numbers are **not** divisors of 100: 90, 72, 33.3, 9, 6, 0*

Multiple

A multiple of an integer N is any integer that is the result of multiplying N with another integer.

Examples
For the number 3, the following are multiples:
-3, 0, 3, 6, 9, 12, 30, 99, 300, 627, 4503

*The following numbers are **not** multiples of 3: 4, 13, 31, 103, 200*

Multiples and factors are related: if N is divisible by integer d, then N is a multiple of d.

Prime Numbers

A prime number is an integer that is divisible by *exactly two* factors: itself and 1.

Prime numbers must be positive, and neither 0 nor 1 is a prime number. Consider:

1 – divisible only by itself. Because itself *is* 1, it only has one factor, and is therefore not prime

0 – 0 is divisible by every integer other than, ironically, itself. When 0 is the dividend, the quotient will always be 0; when 0 is the divisor, the quotient is undefined.

Examples
2, 3, 5, 7, 11, 13, 17, 19, 23, 29, 31 (Memorize these for the GMAT!)

Note

2 is the smallest prime number, and the *only even* prime number (all other even numbers are, by definition, divisible by 2).

> *Facts & Formulas:* If a number is not a prime number, it can be expressed by a set of prime numbers multiplied together (factors).
> $330 = (11) \cdot (5) \cdot (3) \cdot (2)$, $20 = (2) \cdot (2) \cdot (5)$

Divisibility

For quick reference, the following tools are recommended to determine if a dividend is divisible by:

2 – if the dividend is even, it is divisible by 2.

Example:

$$6 \rightarrow \frac{6}{2} = 3 \rightarrow write\ 6\ as\ 3 \cdot 2$$

$$122 \rightarrow \frac{122}{2} = 61 \rightarrow write\ 122\ as\ 61 \cdot 2$$

3 - if the sum of the digits of the dividend is a multiple of 3, then it is divisible by 3.

Example:

$$21 \rightarrow 2 + 1 = 3 \rightarrow \frac{21}{3} = 7 \rightarrow write\ 21\ as\ 7 \cdot 3$$

$$633 \rightarrow 6 + 3 + 3 = 12 \rightarrow \frac{633}{3} = 211 \rightarrow write\ 633\ as\ 211 \cdot 3$$

$$528 \rightarrow 5 + 2 + 8 = 15 \rightarrow \frac{528}{3} = 176 \rightarrow write\ 528\ as\ 176 \cdot 3$$

4 – if the last two digits of the dividend are divisible by 4, then it is divisible by 4.

Example:
724 → 24 is divisible by 4 → write 724 as 181 · 4
892 → 92 is divisible by 4→ write 884 as 223 · 4
2108 → 08 is divisible by 4 → write 2108 as 527 · 4

5 – if the last digit of the dividend is a 5 or a 0, it is divisible by 5.

Example:
35 → ends in 5 → write 35 as 7 · 5
255 → ends in 5 → write 255 as 51 · 5
360 → ends in 0 → write 360 as 72 · 5

6 – if the dividend is even and the sum of its digits is a multiple of 3, it is divisible by 6

Note
This simply combines the rules for 2 and 3, as a number divisible by 6 must be
divisible by the prime factors of 6, which are 2 and 3

9 – if the sum of the digits of the dividend is a multiple of 9, then it is divisible by 9.

Example:
81 → 8 + 1 = 9 → write 81 as 9 · 9
243 → 2 + 4 + 3 = 9 → write 243 as 27 · 9
558 → 5 + 5 + 8 = 18 → write 297 as 62 · 9

10 – if the dividend ends in 0, it is divisible by 10

Example:
0 → ends in 0 → could be written as 0 · 10
420 → ends in 0 → write 420 as 42 · 10

Universal Divisibility Strategy

While other intriguing tricks exist to test divisibility by other numbers, such as 7 and 11, they often require more time to employ and energy to memorize than they are worth. An efficient and useful strategy exists to test for divisibility by any number.

Algebraic theory tells us that:

$a(b+c) = ab + ac$

Similarly:

$7 \cdot 136 = 7(100 + 30 + 6) = 700 + 210 + 42$

Based on this property, in order to test a number such as 952 to determine whether it is divisible by 7, you can simply subtract easy-to-identify multiples of 7 until you reach a recognizable factor or nonfactor of 7. If you reach a factor of 7, or get all the way down to 0, the initial number is divisible by 7; if you reach a nonfactor of 7, then it is not.

For example:

952	
-700	*subtract an easy-to-find multiple of 7*
252	
-210	*again, subtract a multiple of 7*
42	
-42	*once more, subtract a multiple of 7*
0	*because there is no remainder, you can deduce that 952 is divisible by 7*

Please note that this strategy will work for any potential factor.

Consider the example: Is 126 divisible by 4?

126	
-100	*subtract a multiple of 4*
26	
-24	*subtract a multiple of 4*
2	*2 is not divisible by 4, so 126 is not divisible by 4*

For Practice:

1. Is 1386 divisible by 7?

2. Is 727 divisible by 11?

3. Is 559 divisible by 13?

Factoring Drill

Please list the prime factors for each of the following integers:

1. 56

2. 46

3. 36

4. 42

5. 24

6. 81

7. 32

8. 37

9. 124

10. What are **all** the positive factors of 56?

11. What are **all** the positive factors of 42?

12. What are **all** the positive factors of 60?

Divisibility Drill

List the quotient and remainder (if necessary) for each of the following division problems.

1. $79 \div 9$

2. $43 \div 5$

3. $44 \div 3$

4. $41 \div 6$

5. $56 \div 8$

6. $54 \div 8$

7. $23 \div 2$

8. $79 \div 4$

9. $69 \div 7$

10. $39 \div 6$

Answer the following questions.

1. Integer m is greater than 40 but less than 60. If m is divisible by 8, but has a remainder of 2 when divided by 9, what is the value of m?

2. Integer n is divisible by 3. When n is divided by 4, the remainder is 2. What is the value of n if it is greater than 10 but less than 30?

3. If n is divided by either 4 or 5, the remainder is 2. What is the value of n if it is a positive integer less than 40?

Least Common Multiple

When asked to find the least common multiple of two or more integers – a question you may see either explicitly, or as part of a word problem as listed below – the most effective technique is to follow the three-step procedure below:

1. Determine the prime factors of each number

2. Take each prime factor to the highest power in which it appears

3. Multiply together the results of the previous step to form the least common multiple.

Example: What is the least common multiple of 6 and 9?

Prime factors of 6: $2 \cdot 3$
Prime factors of 9: $3 \cdot 3$

Highest power of 2: 2
Highest power of 3: $3 \cdot 3$

Least common multiple of 6 and 9: $2 \cdot 3 \cdot 3 = 18$
18 is the least common multiple of 6 and 9

Note
The same procedure will apply for finding the lowest common denominator of two or more fractions, as you will see later in the lesson.

Word Problem Example:

Widget A has a volume of 6, Widget B has a volume of 8, and Widget C has a volume of 9. If the manufacturer packs only one type of widget in a box and no empty space is required, what is the volume of the smallest box the manufacturer could use if the manufacturer wanted to create a single box to be used no matter which widget is shipped (A, B, or C)?

LCM Drill:

1. What is the least common multiple of 6, 10, and 15?

2. What is the least common multiple of 8, 10, and 12?

3. What is the least common multiple of 5, 8, 12, and 15?

Section Solutions - Divisibility

For Practice:

1. Is 1,386 divisible by 7? Yes.

2. Is 727 divisible by 11? No.

3. Is 559 divisible by 13? Yes.

Factoring Drill

1. 56:   2, 2, 2, 7

2. 46:   2, 23

3. 36:   2, 2, 3, 3

4. 42:   2, 3, 7

5. 24:   2, 2, 2, 3

6. 81:   3, 3, 3, 3

7. 32:   2, 2, 2, 2, 2

8. 37:   37

9. 124:   2, 2, 31

10. What are all the positive factors of 56?

1, 2, 4, 7, 8, 14, 28, 56

11. What are all the positive factors of 42?

1, 2, 3, 6, 7, 14, 21, 42

12. What are all the positive factors of 60?

1, 2, 3, 4, 5, 6, 10, 12, 15, 20, 30, 60

Divisibility Drill

1. $79 \div 9$
8, r 7

2. $43 \div 5$
8, r 3

3. $44 \div 3$
14, r 2

4. $41 \div 6$
6, r 5

5. $56 \div 8$
7 (no remainder)

6. $54 \div 8$
6, r 6

7. $23 \div 2$
11, r 1

8. $79 \div 4$
19, r 3

9. $69 \div 7$
9, r 6

10. $39 \div 6$
6, r 3

1. Integer m is greater than 40 but less than 60. If m is divisible by 8, but has a remainder of 2 when divided by 9, what is the value of m?

Numbers between 40 and 60 that are divisible by 8: 48 and 56
Remainders when divided by 9: 48 → 3; 56 → 2 Answer is 56

2. Integer n is divisible by 3. When n is divisible by 4, the remainder is 2. What is the value of n if it is greater than 10 but less than 30?

Numbers between 10 and 30 that are divisible by 3: 12, 15, 18, 21, 24, 27
Odd numbers will have odd remainders when divisible by an even number, and 12 and 24 are divisible by 4 with no remainder, so the answer is 18.

3. If n is divided by either 4 or 5, the remainder is 2. What is the value of n, if it is a positive interger less than 40?

4 and 5 must divide evenly into n - 2. Thus, n - 2 must be a multiple of both 4 and 5. The only positive interger less than 40 that is a multiple of both 4 and 5 is 20. If n - 2 = 20, then n = 22.

LCM Drill:

1. What is the least common multiple of 6, 10, and 15?
30

2. What is the least common multiple of 8, 10, and 12?
120

3. What is the least common multiple of 5, 8, 12, and 15?
120

Fractions

A fraction is made up of two numbers, a numerator and a denominator: $\dfrac{\text{numerator}}{\text{denominator}}$

and can be interpreted as "numerator divided by denominator".

As the numerator increases the fraction increases.

As the denominator increases the fraction decreases.

Examples of fractions are: $\quad \dfrac{1}{2}, \dfrac{1}{3}, \dfrac{1}{10}, \dfrac{5}{6}, \dfrac{8}{4}, \dfrac{3}{4}, \dfrac{2}{1}, \dfrac{2}{9}, \dfrac{147}{213}, \dfrac{15}{30}, \dfrac{6}{5}$

Exception:
The only number that cannot be part of a fraction is 0 as a denominator because it does not make sense mathematically to divide a number by 0.

> *Facts & Formuals:* The value of a fraction with 0 in the numerator is equal to 0.
>
> The value of a fraction with 1 as a denominator is equal to the value of the numerator.

> *Facts & Formulas:*
>
> 1. Fractions where the numerator is greater than the denominator are equal to a number greater than 1.
>
> 2. Fractions where the numerator is less than the denominator are equal to a number less than 1.
>
> 3. When the numerator is equal to the denominator the fraction is equal to 1.
>
> Assuming $A > B > 0$:
>
> $$\dfrac{A}{B} > 1 \qquad \dfrac{A}{A} = 1 \qquad \dfrac{B}{A} < 1$$

Mixed Numbers

Sometimes a fraction is written as a "mixed number": $2\frac{3}{4}$,

which is to be interpreted as 2 plus the result of 3 divided by 4.

Converting to a normal number:

First calculate the fraction part of the mixed number, and then add it to the normal number part of the mixed number.

$$2\frac{3}{4} \to \frac{3}{4} = 0.75 \to 0.75 + 2 = 2.75$$

If there is a negative sign in front of the mixed number, then both parts of the mixed number are negative:

$$-2\frac{3}{4} = -0.75 - 2 = -2.75$$

Example: $3\frac{1}{2} = 3.5$, $5\frac{1}{3} = 5.33$, $10\frac{1}{10} = 10.1$, $-3\frac{1}{100} = -3.01$, $4\frac{1}{1} = 5$

Converting to a fraction:

Because we are adding two numbers, we must ensure that they have the same denominator. To convert a mixed number to a fraction, we first convert the whole number to a fraction with the same denominator as the fraction, and then add them together.

$$2\frac{3}{4} \to 2 + \frac{3}{4} \to \frac{8}{4} + \frac{3}{4} \to 8 + \frac{3}{4} \to \frac{11}{4}$$

Example: $3\frac{1}{2} = \frac{6}{2} + \frac{1}{2} = \frac{7}{2}$, $5\frac{1}{3} = 15 + \frac{1}{3} = \frac{16}{3}$, $10\frac{1}{10} = \frac{100}{10} + \frac{1}{10} = \frac{101}{10}$

$-3\frac{1}{100} = \frac{300}{100} - \frac{1}{100} = \frac{301}{100}$, $4\frac{1}{1} = \frac{4}{1} + \frac{1}{1} = \frac{5}{1}$

Converting Between Decimals and Fractions

Fractions may be converted to decimals, and vice versa, by remembering that each fraction represents a division problem: numerator divided by denominator. As you likely know, $\frac{1}{2}$ is the same as 0.5, because 1 divided by 2 equals 0.5. Consider that:

$$\frac{1}{2} = 1 \div 2 = 0.5$$

Also:

$$\frac{1}{2} = \frac{5}{10} \text{ or "five tenths", which is the same as } 0.5$$

Converting between fractions and decimals is a particularly useful skill on the GMAT, because you will not be able to use a calculator. Because fractions contain fewer digits than decimals, they are often significantly easier and less time-consuming to use for calculations. Try the problem:

$$.3333 \cdot .1250$$

In decimal form, you would be multiplying together two, four-digit numbers – an incredibly time-consuming process with the potential for error. As fractions, however, the calculation is much easier:

$$\frac{1}{3} \cdot \frac{1}{8} = \frac{1}{24}$$

You will find that the majority of GMAT answer choices will be in either fraction or integer form, and those in decimal form will likely only require an easy-to-solve fraction-to-decimal conversion. Using fractions whenever possible is an efficient strategy to save time and maximize accuracy.

Please complete the following drill, expressing fractions as decimals:

$$\frac{1}{2} = \qquad\qquad\qquad\qquad\qquad \frac{1}{6} =$$

$$\frac{1}{3} = \qquad\qquad\qquad\qquad\qquad \frac{1}{7} =$$

$$\frac{1}{4} = \qquad\qquad\qquad\qquad\qquad \frac{1}{8} =$$

$$\frac{1}{5} = \qquad\qquad\qquad\qquad\qquad \frac{1}{9} =$$

$$\frac{1}{10} =$$

You should notice a pattern in the way that these fractions and decimals interrelate. In order to minimize the amount that you need to memorize, pay attention to these patterns. You should already have memorized:

$$\frac{1}{2} = 0.5$$

$$\frac{1}{3} = 0.333\ldots$$

$$\frac{1}{4} = 0.25$$

$$\frac{1}{5} = 0.2$$

Simply knowing those, you can derive almost all of the remaining fraction conversions:

$$\frac{1}{6} = \frac{1}{3} \cdot \frac{1}{2} = \frac{0.3333}{2} = 0.1667$$

$$\frac{1}{8} = \frac{1}{4} \cdot \frac{1}{2} = \frac{0.25}{2} = 0.125$$

$$\frac{1}{9} = \frac{1}{3} \cdot \frac{1}{3} = \frac{0.3333}{3} = 0.1111$$

The only additional single-digit denominator that you may need to know is $\frac{1}{7}$, which you can memorize as 0.143.

To find other fractions with the same denominator and a different numerator, such as $\frac{4}{9}$, simply multiply the decimal by the numerator, $4 \cdot 0.111 = 0.444$. With other fractions it may be simpler to subtract the decimal from 1.0. For example, $\frac{7}{8}$ is simply $1.0 - .125 = .875$. This technique works best for larger fractions that are closer to 1.

Negative Numbers

If either the numerator or the denominator is negative, the fraction is negative and so is the resulting integer or decimal.

If both the numerator and the denominator are negative, the fraction is positive and so is the resulting integer or decimal.

Reducing Fractions

You will not change the value of a fraction if you multiply or divide the numerator and denominator by the same number.

Think of whole numbers as fractions with a denominator of 1. $5 = \frac{5}{1}$

Example:

$$\frac{1}{3} = \frac{1 \cdot 7}{3 \cdot 7} = \frac{7}{21} = \frac{7 \cdot 2}{21 \cdot 2} = \frac{14}{42} = \frac{\frac{14}{7}}{\frac{42}{7}} = \frac{2}{6}$$

Sometimes fractions may be reduced or simplified by dividing the numerator and denominator by the same number.

$$\frac{313 \div 313}{626 \div 313} = \frac{1}{2}$$

Generally speaking, the most efficient way to reduce a fraction is to break the numerator and denominator down into their respective factors. Continue until you are left with only primes, and look to reduce by factoring out common prime factors. For example:

$$\frac{12}{16} = \frac{4 \cdot 3}{4 \cdot 4} = \frac{2 \cdot 2 \cdot 3}{2 \cdot 2 \cdot 2 \cdot 2}$$

This is then reduced by eliminating numbers that occur both in the numerator and in the denominator, one at a time, until no more numbers can be eliminated:

GMAT Insider: The vast majority of GMAT answer choices are displayed in their simplest forms.

$$\frac{\cancel{2} \cdot 2 \cdot 3}{\cancel{2} \cdot 2 \cdot 2 \cdot 2} = \frac{\cancel{2} \cdot 3}{\cancel{2} \cdot 2 \cdot 2} = \frac{3}{2 \cdot 2} = \frac{3}{4}$$

Multiplication

When multiplying two fractions, simply multiply the two numerators and the two denominators:

$$\frac{2}{3} \cdot \frac{5}{7} = \frac{10}{21}$$

When multiplying a fraction by a whole number, remember that the whole number can be rewritten as a fraction with a denominator as 1, so only multiply the numerator by the whole number:

$$3 \cdot \frac{3}{4} = \frac{3 \cdot 3}{1 \cdot 4} = \frac{9}{4}$$

Division

To divide a fraction by another fraction invert the second fraction and multiply the two fractions. This process may also be described as multiplying by the reciprocal of the divisor.

$$\frac{A}{B} \div \frac{C}{D} = \frac{A}{B} \cdot \frac{D}{C} = \frac{AD}{BC}$$

$$\frac{2}{7} \div \frac{3}{5} = \frac{2}{7} \cdot \frac{5}{3} = \frac{10}{21}$$

$$\frac{3}{5} \div 2 = \frac{3}{5} \div \frac{2}{1} = \frac{3}{5} \cdot \frac{1}{2} = \frac{3}{10}$$

Fraction Manipulation Drill

1. What is the product of the fractions $\frac{275}{32}$ and $\frac{64}{25}$?

2. To what can the fraction $\frac{27}{81}$ be reduced?

3. What number, when divided by $\frac{13}{19}$, equals $\frac{133}{65}$?

4. What is the product of the fractions $\frac{15}{64}$ and $\frac{8}{9}$?

5. What is the result if 84/63 is divided by $\frac{28}{9}$?

6. What is the product of the fractions $\frac{35}{39}$ and $\frac{52}{49}$?

7. What is the result when 99/56 is divided by $\frac{77}{16}$?

8. If the volume of a tank is $\frac{128}{81}$ liters, and the incoming flow rate is 32 liters every 27 hours, how many hours will it take to fill the tank, assuming the process begins when the tank is empty? (For this problem you may need the equation $\text{Rate} = \frac{\text{Quantity}}{\text{Time}}$)

9. If a climber ascends a peak at the rate of 102 meters every 27 minutes, how high will she climb in 18 minutes?

10. What is the product of the fractions $\frac{27}{80}$ and $\frac{35}{63}$?

Addition and Subtraction

In order to add or subtract two fractions, they must have a common denominator.

To find the common denominator multiply the numerator and denominator of each fraction by the denominator of the other fraction.

$$\frac{A}{B} \diagtimes \frac{C}{D} = \frac{AD + BC}{BD}$$

When adding two fractions with a common denominator, the resulting denominator stays

the same while the resulting numerator is the sum of the original two numerators. To see

that this works, try adding $\frac{1}{2} + \frac{1}{2}$ which we know equals 1. $\frac{1}{2} + \frac{1}{2} = \frac{1+1}{2} = \frac{2}{2} = 1$

Example:

$$\frac{1}{2} + \frac{2}{3} = \frac{1 \cdot 3}{2 \cdot 3} + \frac{2 \cdot 2}{3 \cdot 2} = \frac{3}{6} + \frac{4}{6} = \frac{3+4}{6} = \frac{7}{6}$$

When adding more than two fractions, multiply the numerator and denominator of each fraction by the product of all the other fractions' denominators.

$$\frac{1}{2} + \frac{2}{3} + \frac{3}{4} = \frac{1 \cdot 3 \cdot 4}{2 \cdot 3 \cdot 4} + \frac{2 \cdot 2 \cdot 4}{3 \cdot 2 \cdot 4} + \frac{3 \cdot 2 \cdot 3}{4 \cdot 2 \cdot 3} = \frac{12}{24} + \frac{16}{24} + \frac{18}{24} = \frac{12 + 16 + 18}{24} = \frac{46}{24}$$

Subtraction works the exact same way as addition:

$$\frac{1}{2} - \frac{2}{3} - \frac{3}{4} = \frac{1 \cdot 3 \cdot 4}{2 \cdot 3 \cdot 4} - \frac{2 \cdot 2 \cdot 4}{3 \cdot 2 \cdot 4} - \frac{3 \cdot 2 \cdot 3}{4 \cdot 2 \cdot 3} = \frac{12}{24} - \frac{16}{24} - \frac{18}{24} = \frac{12 - 16 - 18}{24} = \frac{22}{24}$$

Lowest Common Denominator

When adding and subtracting fractions you can simplify calculations and save time by finding the lowest common denominator. To do so, recognize that the process of finding the lowest common denominator is the same as finding the least common multiple of the denominators.

As an exercise, please find the lowest common denominator of the fractions:

$$\frac{1}{6} + \frac{5}{8} + \frac{4}{9} + \frac{3}{10} = ?$$

Fraction Addition/Subtraction Drill

1. What is the sum of $\frac{1}{4} + \frac{1}{3} + \frac{1}{6}$?

2. What is the total of $\frac{2}{9} + \frac{1}{4} - \frac{1}{6} + \frac{1}{18}$?

3. What is the total of $\frac{2}{5} - \frac{1}{10} + \frac{3}{4} - \frac{3}{20}$?

Solutions – Fraction Section

Fraction Manipulation Drill

1. What is the product of the fractions $\frac{275}{32}$ and $\frac{64}{25}$?

22

2. To what can the fraction $\frac{27}{81}$ be reduced?

$\frac{1}{3}$

3. What number, when divided by $\frac{13}{19}$, equals 133/65?

$\frac{7}{5}$

4. What is the product of the fractions $\frac{15}{64}$ and $\frac{8}{9}$?

$\frac{5}{24}$

5. What is the result if 84/63 is divided by $\frac{28}{9}$?

$\frac{3}{7}$

6. What is the product of the fractions $\frac{35}{39}$ and $\frac{52}{49}$?

$\frac{20}{21}$

7. What is the result when $\frac{99}{56}$ is divided by $\frac{77}{16}$?

$\frac{18}{49}$

8. If the volume of a tank is $\frac{128}{81}$ liters, and the incoming flow rate is $\frac{32 \text{ liters}}{27 \text{ hours}}$, how many hours will it take to fill the tank, assuming the process begins when the tank is empty? (For this problem you may need the equation Rate $= \frac{\text{Quantity}}{\text{Time}}$)

$\frac{4}{3}$ hours

9. If a climber ascends a peak at the rate of 102 meters every 27 minutes, how high will she climb in 18 minutes?

68 meters

10. What is the product of the fractions $\frac{27}{80}$ and $\frac{35}{63}$?

$\frac{3}{16}$

Fraction Addition/Subtraction Drill

1. What is the sum of $\frac{1}{4} + \frac{1}{3} + \frac{1}{6}$?

$\frac{3}{4}$

2. What is the total of $\frac{2}{9} + \frac{1}{4} - \frac{1}{6} + \frac{1}{18}$?

$\frac{13}{36}$

3. What is the total of $\frac{2}{5} - \frac{1}{10} + \frac{3}{4} - \frac{3}{20}$?

$\frac{9}{10}$

Decimals

Basics

Much like numbers grow by a digit for every tenth power,
> 10, 100, 1,000, 10,000, 100,000, 1,000,000

decimals grow by a digit for every negative tenth power.
> 0.1, 0.01, 0.001, 0.0001, 0.00001, 0.000000

The first digit to the right of the decimal point is called the "tenth".
The second digit to the right of the decimal point is called the "hundredth".
The third digit to the right of the decimal point is called the "thousandth". Etc.

To graphically illustrate how each number is broken up into an infinite number of smaller numbers:

> *Facts & Formulas:* When you multiply a number by ten the decimal point moves one digit to the right. When you divide a number by ten the decimal point moves one digit to the left.
> $65.43 \cdot 10 = 654.3$, $654.3 \cdot 10 = 6543$, $65.43 \div 10 = 6.543$,
> $65.43 \div 1000 = 0.06543$

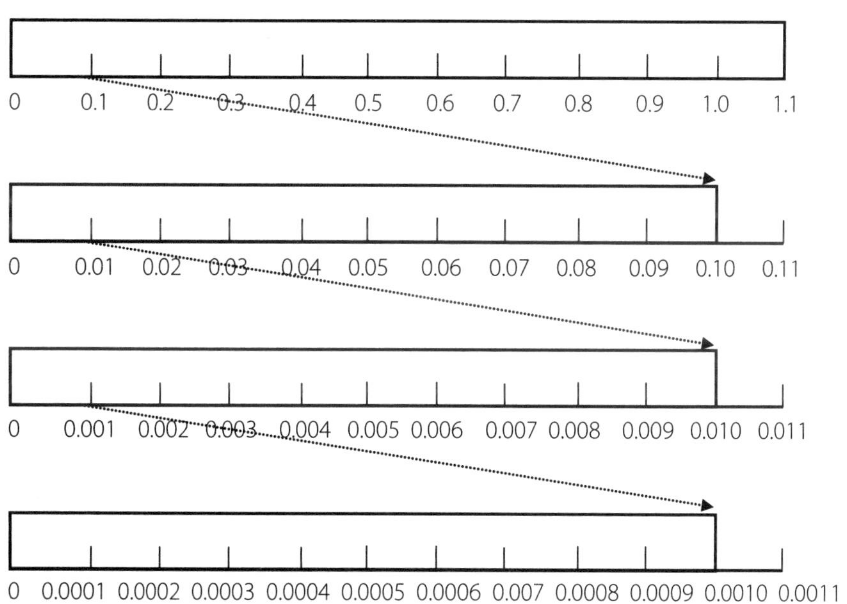

Use of Scientific Notation

Because you cannot use a calculator on the GMAT, calculations involving large, multi-digit numbers may often be more efficiently solved using scientific notation. Such a process sets you up for a quick estimate – be sure to scan the answer choices to see if they are widespread enough to make this an effective strategy, as we will discuss in class – or simpler calculations. The use of scientific notation builds on the concept that:

$$6,000,000 = 6 \cdot 1,000,000$$

And that

$$1,000,000 = 10^6$$

Accordingly, 6,000,000 can be written as $6 \cdot 10^6$.

When conducting calculations that require the use of such large numbers, scientific notation will simplify the math required. Consider the problem:

The board of a hedge fund has decided to divide its $6,000,000 quarterly profits equally among its 12,000 investors. How much will each shareholder receive?

$\dfrac{6,000,000}{12,000}$ can be rewritten as:

$$\frac{6 \cdot 10^6}{12 \cdot 10^3}$$

Using exponent rules (which we will cover extensively later in the algebraic component of this lesson), we can reduce the expression to:

$$\frac{10^3}{2} = 500$$

Therefore, each shareholder will receive $500.

For additional practice with scientific notation, please try the following problem:

Which of the following is closest to the value of $673 \cdot 19,423$?

A) 1,390,000

B) 1,410,000

C) 13,900,000

D) 14,100,000

E) 139,000,000

Rounding

Rounding a decimal number means removing one or more decimal places, while following some specific rules.

If the digit to the right of the decimal place you wish to round to is 4, 3, 2, 1, or 0, simply remove those decimals.

If the digit to the right of the decimal place you wish to round to is 5, 6, 7, 8, or 9, then remove those decimals and add 1 to the decimal place to which you are rounding.

Examples:

  13.2798 → 13.28 Round to the hundredth.

  13.2750001→13.28 Round to the hundredth

  13.27499 → 13.27 Round to the hundredth

  13.27213 → 13.27 Round to the hundredth

  13.2656 → 13.27 Round to the hundredth

  0.454854 → 0.45485 Round to the hundred-thousandth

  0.454854 → 0.4549 Round to the ten-thousandth

  0.454854 → 0.455 Round to the thousandth

  0.454854 → 0.45 Round to the hundredth

  0.454854 → 0.5 Round to the tenth

  0.454854 → 0 Round to a whole number

Note: 0.5 → 1 Round to a whole number

Facts & Formulas: Do <u>not</u> round a number to the desired decimal by rounding one decimal place at a time from the right end of the number. Only evaluate the decimal place <u>immediately</u> to the right of the target decimal place.

Addition and Subtraction

Keep the decimal points lined up under each other. You can always add 0's to the end of a decimal number.

Examples:

$$164.77 + 1.57733 \rightarrow \overset{1\ 1}{164.}77000$$
$$+\ \underline{1.57733}$$
$$=\ 166.34733$$

$$17.9825 - 8.89 \rightarrow \overset{10\ \ 10}{1\!\!7.9825}$$
$$-\ \underline{8.8900}$$
$$=\ 9.0925$$

$$0.01002 + 9 \rightarrow \quad 9.00000$$
$$+\ \underline{0.01002}$$
$$=\ 9.01002$$

$$3.33 - 10.9235 \rightarrow \overset{10\ \ 10}{1\!0.9235}$$
$$-\ \underline{3.3300}$$
$$=\ -7.5935$$

When subtracting a number that is greater than the original number, switch the equation around and put a minus sign in front of the answer.

Multiplication

Multiply as normal, and then place the decimal point so that there are as many decimal places as the sum of the two numbers' decimal places.

Examples

$13.723 \cdot 2.101 \rightarrow$

$$
\begin{array}{r}
13.723 \\
\underline{\times\, 2.101} \\
13723 \\
000000 \\
1372300 \\
\underline{+\, 27446000} \\
= 28.832023
\end{array}
$$

the multiplicand and multiplier each have 3 decimal places $\rightarrow 3 + 3 = 6$

(ignore the decimals during the calculations)

$\leftarrow$ insert 6 decimal places in the product

$5.9 \cdot 0.0872 \rightarrow$

$$
\begin{array}{r}
0.0872 \\
\underline{\times\, 5.9} \\
007848 \\
\underline{+\, 043600} \\
= 0.51448
\end{array}
$$

the multiplicand and multiplier have 4 and 1 decimal places $\rightarrow 4 + 1 = 5$

Memorize the following: **Multiplication Table**

	1	2	3	4	5	6	7	8	9	10
1	1									
2	2	4								
3	3	6	9							
4	4	8	12	16						
5	5	10	15	20	25					
6	6	12	18	24	30	36				
7	7	14	21	28	35	42	49			
8	8	16	24	32	40	48	56	64		
9	9	18	27	36	45	54	63	72	81	
10	10	20	30	40	50	60	70	80	90	100

> *Facts & Formulas:* When multiplying two numbers, most often it is more efficient to list the one with the fewest digits underneath. In certain situations, however, the strategy may change. Look for opportunities to include multiple occurrences of 0, 1, and 2, as well as repeating digits, in the lower row to minimize your number of calculations.

Division

It is not possible to divide by a decimal number without adjusting both the divisor and the dividend. Follow these steps:

i)   In the dividend, move the decimal place to the right as many digits as there are decimal places in the divisor. If there are not enough decimal places in the dividend, add zeros.

ii)   Remove the decimal point from the divisor.

iii)   Divide as usual.

iv)   Place a decimal point in the answer at the same decimal place as it is in the dividend.

> **Facts & Formulas:** If the dividend is smaller than the divisor, add 0's behind the decimal point of the dividend.

Examples

$152.56 \div 9.535 \rightarrow$ *i) $152.56 \rightarrow 152560$*

(there are three decimal places in 9.535)
ii) $9.535 \rightarrow 9535$

$$iii)\ 9535\overline{)152560}$$
$$\underline{9535}$$
$$57210$$
$$57210$$

with quotient 16.

iv) There are no decimals in the dividend. The answer is 16.

$18.42 \div 6 \rightarrow$ *i) 18.42   (there are no decimal places in 6)*

ii) 6

$$iii)\ 6\overline{)18.42}$$

with quotient 307.

$$\underline{18}$$
$$42$$
$$\underline{42}$$

iv) There are two decimals in the dividend. The answer is 3.07.

$68 \div 272 \rightarrow$

$$272\overline{)68.00}$$

$$\begin{array}{r} 25 \\ \underline{544} \\ 1360 \\ \underline{1360} \end{array}$$

Add two zeros because one zero is not sufficient (it leaves a remainder of 136). Two zeros leaves no remainder.

The answer is 0.25

Decimal Calculation Drill

1. What is the fraction $\frac{4}{9}$ expressed as a decimal?

2. $\dfrac{40,000}{0.05} \cdot \dfrac{3}{100} =$

3. The product of $\dfrac{900}{0.00005}$ and $\dfrac{0.25}{0.03}$ is what?

4. If $\dfrac{17,000}{20}$ is multiplied by $\dfrac{6,000}{510}$, what is the result?

5. What is the result if 0.0777 is multiplied by $\dfrac{990}{7}$?

6. What is the result if $\dfrac{0.00667}{800}$ is divided by $\dfrac{0.025}{3,000}$

Solutions – Decimal Section

Use of Scientific Notation:

Which of the following is closest to the value of $673 \cdot 19{,}423$?

C) 13,900,000

Decimal Calculation Drill

1. What is the fraction $\frac{4}{9}$ expressed as a decimal?

0.444…

2. $\dfrac{40{,}000}{0.05} \cdot \dfrac{3}{100} =$

24,000

3. The product of $\dfrac{900}{0.00005}$ and $\dfrac{0.25}{0.03}$ is what?

150,000,000

4. If $\dfrac{17{,}000}{20}$ is multiplied by $\dfrac{6{,}000}{510}$, what is the result?

10,000

5. What is the result if 0.0777 is multiplied by $\dfrac{990}{7}$?

11

6. What is the result if $\dfrac{0.00667}{800}$ is divided by $\dfrac{0.025}{3{,}000}$?

1

Percentages

Percentages are indicative of many of the items you will see on the GMAT in that they seem relatively straightforward – and, as we will demonstrate, they can be – but tend to be presented in precisely the right way as to cause trouble for a large number of examinees. In other words, test-takers often underestimate the difficulty of percentage problems and the number of forms they can take, and will often unknowingly miss questions as a result.

Mathematicians will often remark at the beauty of math problem, in that they can be approached in multiple ways, but will always produce the correct answers (when done correctly, of course). Percentages are no exception – in fact, percentages exemplify that point quite readily. In several chapters of this lesson, we will focus on a simple strategy that will allow you to navigate percentage and word problems efficiently and accurately by translating the GMAT's words directly to operations. While each of these problems may well be solved by a variety of other methods, we highly recommend this strategy as a regimented approach that will save you time and mental energy in the long run.

The Language of Mathematics

Often called "the universal language", mathematics features a number of operations that translate directly into words – and more importantly, the inverse is true, as well. In many questions, the GMAT will present you with problems in word form, and require you to form the appropriate mathematical relationships and complete the subsequent calculations. Be advised that the vast majority of the words provided will translate directly into the equations and relationships that they represent, allowing you to quickly transition to calculations. Consider the question:

What is 20% of 15?

Each word, number, or symbol in the above statement has a direct mathematical equivalent:

What → the unknown, and can be represented as a variable, x
Is → equality, and can be represented as =
20 → 20
% → percent, which can be broken into two components:
Per → divided by, represented as ÷
Cent → 100
Of → multiplied by, represented as ·

$$15 \rightarrow 15$$

Accordingly, our equation is essentially given to us directly in the sentence:

$$x = \frac{20}{100} \cdot 15$$

$$x = \frac{1}{5} \cdot 15 = 3$$

Important Translations For Percentage Problems

what $\rightarrow x$ is $\rightarrow =$ of $\rightarrow \cdot$

per $\rightarrow \div$ increases by $\rightarrow +$ decreases by $\rightarrow -$

Percent $\rightarrow /100$

Of these word-to-operation conversions, two stand out as paramount to your understanding of percentage problems:

1) Percent means "fraction of 100", or /100

By treating all percentages as fractions, rather than decimals, you will find yourself in a great position to take advantage of the fact that fractions often reduce to small, easy-to-manipulate values. In this way, 25% becomes ¼, 20% becomes 1/5, and so on – you will note that the majority of percentage problems you see on the GMAT will feature well-designed sets of numbers that will reduce rather quickly to simple numbers when you choose to focus on fractions.

Example: *What is 60% of 75?*

$$x = \frac{60}{100} \cdot 75$$ *(convert words to operations)*

$$x = \frac{3}{5} \cdot 75$$ *(reduce the fraction)*

$$x = \frac{(3 \cdot 75)}{5}$$ *(combine both numerators)*

$$x = 3 \cdot 15$$ *(divide 75 by 5, reducing the fraction further)*

$$x = 45$$ *(complete the operations to solve for x)*

2) Percentages must be taken "of" a value

Percentages don't exist on their own – they must represent a fraction of an existing value. Perhaps the single greatest mistake that examinees make with percent questions is that they often take the percentage of the incorrect value. When taking a percentage, ask yourself the question "of what?" so that you organize your thoughts appropriately. Consider the example below.

Example: *25 increases by 20%*

$$25 + \frac{20}{100}\cdots$$

The 20% must be a fraction of a value; in this case, it's a fraction of itself

25 increases by 20% (of itself)

$$25 + \frac{20}{100} \cdot 25$$

$$25 + \frac{1}{5} \cdot 25$$

$$25 + \frac{25}{5}$$

$$25 + 5 = 30$$

Percent Increases and Decreases

Increases by $\rightarrow +$

Decreases by $\rightarrow -$

Examples:

10 increases by 20%

$$10 + \frac{20}{100} \cdot 10$$

$$10 + \frac{1}{5} \cdot 10$$

$$10 + \frac{10}{5}$$

$$10 + 2 = 12$$

20 decreases by 40%

$$20 - \frac{40}{100} \cdot 20$$

$$20 - \frac{2}{5} \cdot 20$$

$$20 - \frac{(2 \cdot 20)}{5}$$

$$20 - (2 \cdot 4) = 20 - 8 = 12$$

Calculating Percentages

Take the question "a is what percent of b?"

Again, use the language of mathematics to set up your calculation

$$a = \frac{x}{100} \cdot b$$

Example:
32 is what percent of 40?
$$32 = \frac{x}{100} \cdot 40$$

The "language of mathematics" method will provide you with a logical setup for these questions, but simply setting up a ratio may save you a step or two. Thinking that way, you could rephrase the statement as:

32 out of 40 is what fraction of 100?

$$\frac{32}{40} = \frac{x}{100}$$

Please note that this ratio is formed simply by taking one algebraic step past the "language of mathematics" method above. The initial method will always set you up with an efficient, logical equation, but, as discussed earlier, the beauty of mathematics is that there are multiple accurate paths to the correct answer.

Percentage Drill

1. What is 30% of 30?

2. What is 40% of 40?

3. What is 36% of 50?

4. 18 increases by 50%

5. 40 increases by 20%

6. 35 decreases by 40%

7. 75 decreases by 16%

8. 36 increases by 150%

9. 16 increases by 125%

10. What is 126% of 50?

11. 12 is what percent of 60?

12. 99 is what percent of 132?

Percent Change

$$\% \text{ change} = \frac{(\text{New Value} - \text{Original Value})}{\text{Original Value}} \cdot 100$$

Example: If a $5 investment grows to $6, by what percent does it increase?

$$\% \text{ change} = \frac{(6\text{-}5)}{5} \cdot 100$$
$$= \frac{1}{5} \cdot 100$$
$$= \frac{100}{5} = 20\%$$

Note the logic in the equation:

- Whether the change is an increase or decrease will be reflected in whether the result takes a positive or negative sign

- The statement "by what percent does it increase" requires the percentage to be taken "of" a value; it is natural that it will change by a factor of what it originally was (Original Value)

- Multiplying by 100 simply turns the fraction $\left(\frac{1}{5}\right)$ into a percentage – the same could be done by arranging a ratio: $\frac{1}{5} = \frac{x}{100}$. In this case, to solve for x, you would simply multiply both sides by 100, and end up with $\frac{100}{5} = 20$

Try the following examples to apply the formula for yourself:

1. What is the percent change if 5 grows to 8?

2. What is the percent change if 5 is reduced to 3?

Percentage Change Drill

In this drill, first determine "of" which value the percentage will be taken, then solve for the percent change.

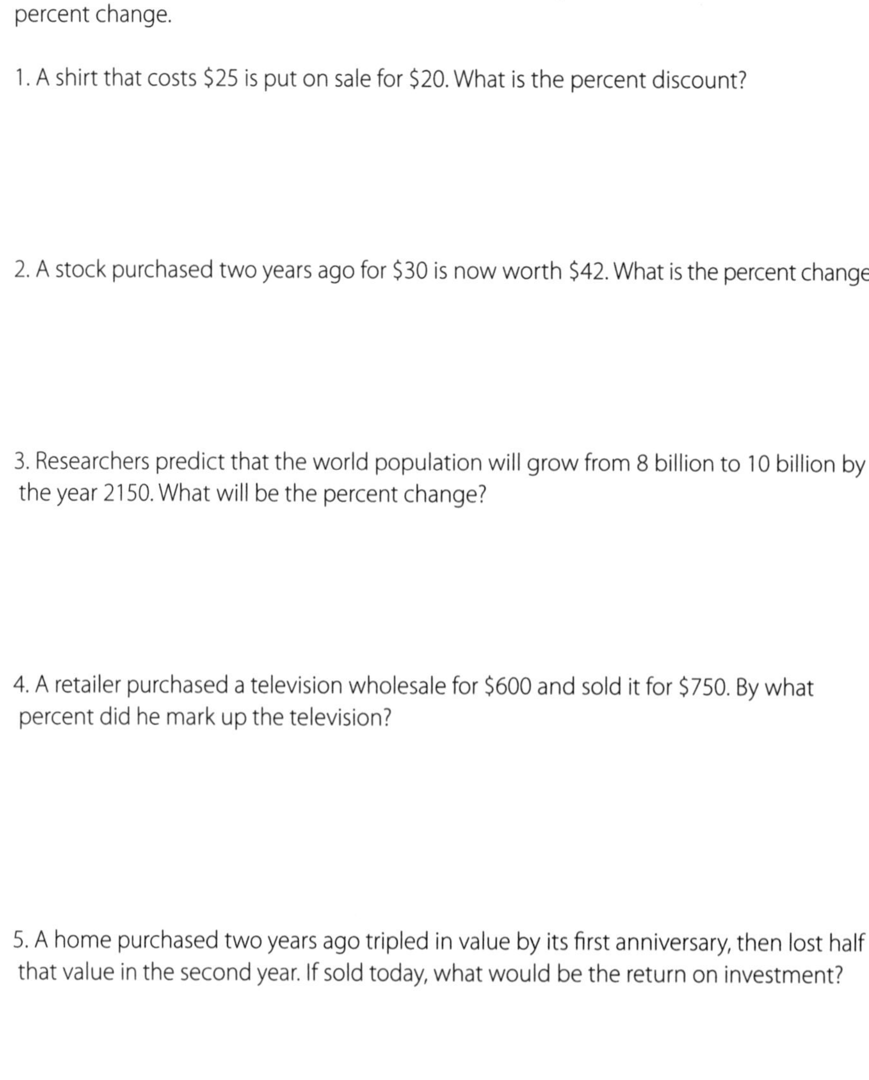

1. A shirt that costs $25 is put on sale for $20. What is the percent discount?

2. A stock purchased two years ago for $30 is now worth $42. What is the percent change?

3. Researchers predict that the world population will grow from 8 billion to 10 billion by the year 2150. What will be the percent change?

4. A retailer purchased a television wholesale for $600 and sold it for $750. By what percent did he mark up the television?

5. A home purchased two years ago tripled in value by its first anniversary, then lost half that value in the second year. If sold today, what would be the return on investment?

Percentage Word Problems

1. On a plane there are a total of 400 seats, 24 of which are first class. What percent of the seats are first class?

2. In a bank, 22% of the value of all the money consists of ten-dollar bills. There are 600 million dollars in the bank. What is the total value of the ten-dollar bills?

3. A rugby team has won 12 games, or 75% of total games played, during the season. How many games have they played during the season?

4. A stock is worth \$20 on January 15th, 2001. A year later it has grown by 50%. The following year it falls 50%. On January 15th, 2003, how many percent has the value of the stock increased or decreased since January 15th, 2001?

Solutions – Percentage Section

1. What is 30% of 30?

9

2. What is 40% of 40?

16

3. What is 36% of 50?

18

4. 18 increases by 50%

27

5. 40 increases by 20%

48

6. 35 decreases by 40%

21

7. 75 decreases by 16%

63

8. 36 increases by 150%

90

9. 16 increases by 125%

36

10. What is 126% of 50?

63

11. 12 is what percent of 60?

20

12. 99 is what percent of 132?

75

Percentage Change Drill

1. A shirt that costs $25 is put on sale for $20. What is the percent discount?

The original value is $25, and the new value is $20, so we will use the equation:

$$\% \text{ change} = \frac{(20-25)}{25} * 100$$

$$\% \text{ change} = -\frac{5}{25} * 100$$

$$\% \text{ change} = -\frac{1}{5} * 100 = -20$$

20% decrease

2. A stock purchased two years ago for $30 is now worth $42. What is the percent change?

The original value is $30 and the new value is $42, so we will use the equation:

$$\% \text{ change} = \frac{(42-30)}{30} * 100$$

$$\% \text{ change} = \frac{12}{30} * 100$$

$$\% \text{ change} = \frac{2}{5} * 100 = 40$$

40% increase

3. Researchers predict that the world population will grow from 8 billion to 10 billion by the year 2150. What will be the percent change?

The original value is 8 billion and the new value is 10 billion, so we will use the equation:

$$\% \text{ change} = \frac{(10-8)}{8} * 100$$

$$\% \text{ change} = \frac{2}{8} * 100$$

$$\% \text{ change} = \frac{1}{4} * 100 = 25$$

25% increase

4. A retailer purchased a television wholesale for $600 and sold it for $750. By what percent did he mark up the television?

The original value is $600 and the new value is $750, so we will use the equation:

$$\% \text{ change} = \frac{(750-600)}{600} \cdot 100$$

$$\% \text{ change} = \frac{150}{600} \cdot 100 = \frac{1}{4} \cdot 100 = 25$$

25% increase

5. A home purchased two years ago tripled in value by its first anniversary, then lost half that value in the second year. If sold today, what would be the return on investment?

The original price is a variable, which we can call p. In the first year, it tripled, making that value 3p, and in the second year it was reduced by half of the 3p value, making the new value $\frac{3p}{2}$. We will use the formula:

$$\% \text{ change} = \frac{\left(\frac{3p}{2} - p\right)}{p} \cdot 100$$

$$\% \text{ change} = \frac{\left(\frac{p}{2}\right)}{p} \cdot 100 = \frac{1}{2} \cdot 100 = 50$$

50% increase

Percentage Word Problems

1. On a plane there are a total of 400 seats, 24 of which are first class. How many percent of the seats are first class?

Setting this problem up using the "language of mathematics", we can phrase it as "24 is what percent of 400", or:

$$24 = \frac{x}{100} \cdot 400 \qquad \text{(translate words into mathematics)}$$

$$24 = \frac{400x}{100} \qquad \text{(simplify the expression)}$$

$$24 = 4x \qquad \text{(factor out the fraction)}$$

$$6 = x \qquad \text{(divide both sides by 4 to isolate x)}$$

2. In a bank, 22% of the value of all the money consists of ten-dollar bills. There are 600 million dollars in the bank. What is the total value of the ten-dollar bills?

Setting this problem up mathematically, we can use the phrase "what is 22% of 600?":

$$x = \frac{22}{100} \cdot 600 \qquad \text{(translate words into mathematics)}$$

$$x = 22 \cdot \frac{600}{100} \qquad \text{(simplify the expression)}$$

$$x = 22 \cdot 6 \qquad \text{(factor out the fraction)}$$

$$x = 132 \text{ million dollars} \qquad \text{(carry out the calculations)}$$

3. A rugby team has won 12 games, or 75% of total games played, during the season. How many games have they played during the season?

Setting up this problem mathematically, we can say that "12 is 75% of the total":

$$12 = \frac{75}{100} \cdot T \qquad \text{(translate words into mathematics)}$$

$$12 = \frac{3}{4} \cdot T \qquad \text{(factor out the fraction)}$$

$$12 \cdot \frac{4}{3} = T \qquad \text{(multiply both sides by } \frac{3}{4} \text{ to isolate T)}$$

$$16 = T \rightarrow 16 \text{ total games played} \qquad \text{(carry out the calculations)}$$

4. A stock is worth \$20 on January 15th, 2001. A year later it has grown by 50%. The following year it falls 50%. On January 15th, 2003, how many percent has the value of the stock increased or decreased since January 15th, 2001?

We can begin by taking the stock's first change – a \$20 stock grows by 50% (of itself):

$$20 + \frac{50}{100} \cdot 20 = 20 + 10 = 30$$

Then, the new \$30 stock decreases by 50% (of itself):

$$30 - \frac{50}{100} \cdot 30 = 30 - 15 = 15$$

Then, we calculate the percentage change, using the original value of \$20 and the new value of \$15:

$$\% \text{ change} = \frac{(15\text{-}20)}{20} \cdot 100$$

$$\% \text{ change} = \frac{-5}{20} \cdot 100$$

$$\% \text{ change} = -\frac{1}{4} \cdot 100 = -25$$

25% decrease

Simplifying Calculations

You will note that extensive calculations are very rarely required on the GMAT. As we have seen previously when considering fractions and percentages, the GMAT is constructed so that a significant competitive advantage exists for those who can identify a simpler way to perform calculations.

The following are advanced strategies for solving seemingly difficult questions more quickly:

1) Break one difficult calculation into two simple calculations:

Example: $97 + 237 \rightarrow 100 + 234 = 334$

By adding 3 to the first number and subtracting the same 3 from the second, we create an easy-to-use factor of 10 that makes mental addition possible.

2) Choose the order of calculation:

Example: $2 \cdot 2 \cdot 2 \cdot 3 \cdot 3 \cdot 5 \rightarrow 2 \cdot 5 \cdot 2 \cdot 2 \cdot 3 \cdot 3 \rightarrow 10 \cdot 4 \cdot 9 = 360$

By reordering the order in which we multiply the same set of numbers, we can find simpler calculations.

Lazy Genius: Often, the easiest way to perform any calculation is to look for the opportunity to create factors of 10. Numbers with units digits of 10 are easier to manipulate than others.

Algebra

A favorite topic of the GMAT – officially, 25% of quantitative problems are deemed "algebra problems", but you'll likely find that closer to half of the problems you see will require algebra in some form – algebra refers to the process of identifying unknown quantities. Its parallels to business are clear – in both algebra and business, you will seek to apply your resources to accomplish greater goals, and obtain even more resources. Algebraically, this is accomplished by leveraging your known quantities to solve for variables. In its most basic form, algebra involves:

1) Assigning variables for unknowns

What number, when increased by 4, will produce 6?

The "what number" portion is the unknown quantity that we seek to identify; by assigning it a variable, such as x, we can express the question mathematically:

$$x + 4 = 6$$

Similarly, if we wanted to know what number, when multiplied by 3, produces a value six greater than itself, we could call that value 'x' in both places (multiplied by 3 and added to 6):

What number multiplied by 3 equals six greater than itself: $\qquad x \cdot 3 = 6 + x$

2) Creating and manipulating equations – and inequalities – to isolate and solve for variables

We will cover inequalities later in the lesson, and for now focus on equations. Manipulating equations to solve for variables is a skill of primary importance on the GMAT, and stems from the fact that:

= means "is identical to"

> *GMAT Insider:* When assigning variables, you can choose any letter you wish, but be strategic; avoid using letters such as o, l, and i that you may confuse for numbers, and choose variables that correspond to the unknowns whenever possible (h = height, d = distance, etc.)

Because of that, in the examples above:

$x + 4 = 6 \rightarrow x + 4$ is another way to represent the exact value of 6 – anything you could do to the number 6, you could do to the expression $x + 4$ and it would respond the same way as 6 would.

In essence, saying that $x + 4 = 6$ is the same as saying $6 = 6$. And if both sides of the equation are identical, you can manipulate them the same way:

If we add two to both:	$6 = 6$ becomes $6 + 2 = 6 + 2$	$8 = 8$
If we multiply both by 2:	$6 \cdot 2 = 6 \cdot 2$	$12 = 12$
If we square both:	$6^2 = 6^2$	$36 = 36$
If we divide the squares by 2:	$\dfrac{6^2}{2} = \dfrac{6^2}{2}$	$18 = 18$

Once we know that two expressions are identical, as long as we perform the same operation to each of the two expressions, we will preserve that equality. Because we have determined in our equation that $x + 4$ is the same as 6, we can treat both expressions as exactly the same and perform the same
operations above to both:

Add two to both: $x + 4 + 2 = 6 + 2$

Multiply both by 2: $(x + 4) \cdot 2 = 6 \cdot 2$

Note: because the expression $x + 4$ is equal to 6, we must multiply the entire expression by 2, and not simply one portion of it.

Square both: $(x + 4)^2 = 6^2$

Divide both squares by 2: $\dfrac{(x + 4)^2}{2} = \dfrac{6^2}{2}$

Strategically, however, our goal is to determine what x represents, and we'll want to manipulate the equation accordingly. Because we know the value of $x + 4$, and want to get x on its own, it makes strategic sense to subtract 4 from both expressions to identify x:

Initial equation: $x + 4 = 6$

Subtract four from both: $x + 4 - 4 = 6 - 4$

The result: $x = 2$

Another example:

Initial equation: $3x + 5 = 20$

Subtract five from both $3x + 5 - 5 = 20 - 5$

Result: $3x = 15$

Divide both by three: $\dfrac{3x}{3} = \dfrac{15}{3}$

Result: $x = 5$

As demonstrated above, your basic, guiding principles of algebra should be:

1) Use the definition of "equals" – also represented by "is" and its many conjugations (was, were, are, will be, etc.) – to construct and manipulate equations.

2) Be sure to perform the same calculations to each expression – it is the entire side of the equation that equals the other, and so you must perform each operation to the entire expression, and not one individual term.

3) Strategically perform operations to isolate your variable on one side of the equation so that you can solve for a single quantity.

Keeping those principles in mind, algebra on the GMAT will be designed to look intimidating – featuring exponents, roots, multiple variables, etc. – but will always have the same goal: solve for unknowns. In this lesson, you will learn the many types of operations you can (and cannot) perform to solve for variables, and the multiple types of equations (and inequalities) that you will face. The following is a list of what we will cover in this lesson:

- The ultimate goal: Solving for variables

- Rules for Operations
    - What may and may not be Added or Subtracted
    - Order when Adding or Multiplying
    - Variable multiplied by itself
    - Parentheses
    - Order when carrying out *different* operations

- Solving equations
    - Simplifying expressions
    - Solving for multiple variables
    - Dealing with absolute values

- Inequalities

- Solving equations that include exponentials
    - Exponentials
    - Roots
    - Factoring
    - Quadratic formula

- Word Problems
    - Conversions
    - Translating English into mathematics

Algebraic Definitions

Variables are unknowns, represented by letters such as x, y, z, a, b, or c.

Coefficients are the numbers in front of variables, and denote that the variable is multiplied by that number:

The coefficient of 9x is 9, and the expression means "9 times x"

The coefficient of $3y^2$ is 3, and the expression means "3 times (y-squared)"

Even the expression z has a coefficient – the one is implied ("one times z")

Addition and Subtraction

One cannot add unlike terms. That is, one cannot add:
- an unknown variable with a number, a + 1
- two different variables, a + b
- two like variables of different powers, $a + a^2$

One can add like terms. Do so by combining coefficients:
- 3x + 5x = 8x
- 9y – y = 8y

Examples:
$4x + 3 + 2x - 1 = 6x + 2$
$x^2 + 2y + 2y - 3 - y^2 + 4 - x^2 - x \longrightarrow -y^2 + 4y - x + 1$

Drill:

1. Simplify 3x – y + 2x + 9y

2. Simplify $3x^2 + 4x + 5x^2 + 6x$

3. Simplify x + y + z – x + y + z

GMAT Insider: Perhaps the trickiest coefficient of all is -1 (negative one) – because the coefficient of 1 is typically implied as seen above, examinees often forget to multiply -1 as the coefficient of an algebraic term. When approaching such a situation, be sure to specify the -1 coefficient in your notes to avoid such a mistake.

Order and Grouping

When adding or multiplying numbers, the following properties will hold, which may make your calculations easier:

Commutative Property

When adding or multiplying numbers and/or variables, the order of the terms does not change the results – addition or multiplication can be done in any order and produce the same result. Based on the commutative property, you can "commute" additive or multiplicative terms throughout the expression without changing the result.

$$B \cdot A \cdot 2 = B \cdot 2 \cdot A = 2AB$$
$$100 \cdot 8 = 8 \cdot 100$$
$$100 + 8 = 8 + 100$$

Associative Property

When adding or multiplying groups of numbers and/or variables, the way in which they are grouped does not change the outcome. Based on the associative property, you can associate variables or numbers together in any grouping without changing the result:

$$2 \cdot (A \cdot B) = (2 \cdot A) \cdot B = 2 \cdot A \cdot B = 2AB$$
$$2 \cdot (10 \cdot 6) = (2 \cdot 10) \cdot 6 = 120$$
$$2 + (10 + 6) = (2 + 10) + 6 = 18$$

Again, this will only hold when dealing with one type of operation, either multiplication or addition. When multiple operations are present, the associative property will not hold.

Facts & Formulas: When a problem includes multiple operations, such as multiplication and addition, the commutative property will not hold; only use this property when dealing solely with one type of operation, either addition or multiplication.

GMAT Insider: Equations on the GMAT are often constructed to appear less manageable than they are. Use of the commutative and associative properties can help you rearrange the equations to better see relationships between variables and numbers. When an algebraic expression looks difficult, try rearranging the terms for a fresh perspective.

Multiplication

When multiplying two **different** variables or a number and a variable, neither term disappears nor do new variables or numbers appear. The convention is simply to place them next to each other. $a \cdot b = ab$

Examples
$5 \cdot x = 5x$
$x \cdot y \cdot z = xyz$
$x^2 \cdot 4 \cdot z = 4x^2z$
$2 \cdot z \cdot x \cdot y \cdot 3 = 6xyz$

> *Facts & Formulas:* As the commutative property notes, the order of terms in a multiplication expression is irrelevant. $2ab = b2a$

Multiplying two **like** variables results in a single variable raised to the power of the sum of the powers of the variables being multiplied. $a^1 \cdot a^2 = a^{1+2} = a^3$

Examples
$x \cdot x \cdot 5 = 5x^2$
$x \cdot x \cdot y \cdot x \cdot z \cdot y = x^3y^2z$
$x^3 \cdot x^2 = x^5$
$5 \cdot x^4 \cdot 2 \cdot y \cdot y^2 \cdot x = 10x^5y^3$
$4x^3 \cdot \dfrac{2}{x^5} = 4x^3 \cdot 2x^{-5} = 8x^{3-5} = 8x^{-2}$

> *Facts & Formulas:* The power of a number expresses how many times a number is multiplied by itself. Negative powers signify that the variable is a denominator.
>
> $x^0 = 1$, $x^1 = x$, $x^{-1} = \dfrac{1}{x}$, $x^{-y} = \dfrac{1}{x^y}$, $x^3 = x \cdot x \cdot x$, $x^{-3} = \dfrac{1}{x^3}$

Distributive Property

When multiplication involves an expression in parentheses, the multiplication must be distributed to each term within the parentheses:

$2(x + y) = 2x + 2y$

For a demonstration, let's go back to our initial equation that $x + 4 = 6$, and distribute multiplication to both sides simultaneously. Remember that when we solved for x, we determined that $x = 2$. For this demonstration, we will multiply by 2:

$2(2 + 4) = 2(6)$	initial equation	$2(x + 4) = 2(6)$
$2 \cdot 2 + 2 \cdot 4 = 12$	distribute multiplication	$2x + 2 \cdot 4 = 12$
$4 + 8 = 12$	perform multiplication	$2x + 8 = 12$
		$\underline{ -8 \quad -8}$
$12 = 12$	add/subtract numbers	$2x \quad = 4$
	solve for x	$x = 2$

We see on the left that distributing the multiplication preserves the equality – if we split up 6 into 2 + 4, we need to multiply the coefficient by both terms in order for both to correctly equal 12.

On the right, we see that using the distributive property allows us to isolate the variable, x, by eliminating the parentheses, and we can accordingly perform the necessary operations to correctly deduce that x = 2.

Examples:
$A \cdot (B + C) = A \cdot B + A \cdot C$
$3 \cdot (12 + 7) = (3 \cdot 12) + (3 \cdot 7)$
$5(x + y) = 5x + 5y$
$6(3 + x) = 6 \cdot 3 + 6x = 18 + 6x$

Division

When dividing two **different** variables or a number and a variable, neither term disappears nor do any new variables or numbers appear. The convention is simply to place the dividend in the numerator and the divisor in the denominator.

Examples:

$$5 \div x = \frac{5}{x}$$

$$x \div yz = \frac{x}{yz}$$

When dividing two **like** variables, you can think of it as multiplying variables where the variables in the denominator have negative powers. $\frac{a}{a} = a^1 \cdot a^{-1} = a^0 = 1$

Examples:

$$\frac{x^3}{x^2} = x^{3-2} = x^1 = x$$

$$\frac{x^2 y}{yz} = x^2 y^{1-1} z^1 = x^2 y^0 z^1 = \frac{x^2}{z}$$

$$\frac{8yx^3}{2x^2} = 4yx$$

$$\frac{6x^4 y}{2y^2 x} = 3x^{4-1} y^{1-2} = \frac{3x^3}{y}$$

Order of Operations

When facing an expression that involves multiple expressions, it is important to perform them in the correct order in order to obtain the correct answer. As we have seen via the distributive property:

$2(2 + 4) = 2(6) = 12$ (add within the parentheses, then multiply)
Or
$2(2 + 4) = 2 \cdot 2 + 2 \cdot 4 = 4 + 8 = 12$ (distribute multiplication, then combine)
But Not
$2 \cdot 2 + 4 = 4 + 4 = 8$ ~~(multiply before eliminating parentheses)~~

Already we know that parentheses take precedence, or otherwise we'll end up with an incorrect expression. Parentheses must be handled first in any expression, as they denote that the entire term contained within them is taken as one entity. The rest of the operations are handled in the order:

1) Parentheses
2) Exponents
3) Multiplication
4) Division
5) Addition
6) Subtraction

Because multiplication and division, like addition and subtraction, are essentially identical operations, either can be handled in either order (multiplying by 2 is the same as dividing by $\frac{1}{2}$, and subtracting 2 is the same as adding -2). The above list, however, forms the oft-used acroynym "PEMDAS", or "Please Excuse My Dear Aunt Sally", which makes for quick recognition.

Examples:
$2 \cdot 3 + 4 =$
$a.\ 2 \cdot 7 \quad b.\ 6 + 4$

$6 \div 3 + 3 =$
$a.\ 2 + 3 \quad b.\ 6 \div 6$

$5 \cdot (2 + 3) =$
$a.\ 10 + 3 \quad b.\ 5 \cdot 5$

Multiple Parentheses

When an expression has multiple sets of parentheses, begin by working with the innermost set of parentheses and work your way out. Take, for example, the expression:

$2(3 + 4(3 - 1))$

You would begin by eliminating the innermost parentheses, which surround the expression (3-1):

$2(3 + 4(2))$
$2(3 + 8)$

Then, with only one set of parentheses left, you can either distribute the multiplication, or perform the operation within the parentheses. In this case, simply adding the terms within the parentheses will likely be easier:

$2(11) = 22$

Another example:

$x^3(1 + 3(x + 2 - y^2(xy - 3x^2)) - y)$

Please visit Veritas Prep on Demand for a detailed, step-by-step analysis of this example.

More Order of Operations – Denominators

An additional operation common to GMAT problems is the use of multi-component denominators. An example:

$$\frac{3}{(2+x)} = \frac{4}{(3+x)}$$

Note that, as seen in this example, a denominator with multiple components signifies that the numerator is divided by that entire term – 3/(2+x) means three divided by the expression 2+x as a whole. Accordingly, these denominators, although they signify division, should be treated as parenthetical expressions – more often than not, multiplying to eliminate denominators is a logical first step, as it simplifies the equation dramatically from the beginning.

The procedure for eliminating denominators is the same as we have used for manipulating any algebraic equation – we must perform the same operation to each side of the equation:

$$\frac{3}{(2+x)} = \frac{4}{(3+x)}$$

We can start by eliminating the denominator on the left side of the equation; to do so, we will want to multiply each side by the entire denominator, (2+x)

$$(2+x) \cdot \frac{3}{(2+x)} = 4 \cdot \frac{(2+x)}{(3+x)}$$

The (2+x) terms on the left will cancel, leaving us with:

$$3 = 4\frac{(2+x)}{(3+x)}$$

Next, we'll want to eliminate the denominator on the right side, again peforming the same operation – multiplying by (3+x) – on both sides:

$$3(3+x) = (3+x) \cdot \frac{4(2+x)}{(3+x)}$$

The (3+x) terms on the right will cancel, leaving us with a simplified expression:

$$3(3+x) = 4(2+x)$$

Before we solve for x, it is important to note that this process of eliminating denominators can be streamlined through a process called "cross-multiplying".

Cross Multiplication

In the problem on the previous page, our process was to multiply each side by both denominators. In this way, each side's numerator would factor with its own denominator, and we'd be left with the equation:

$3(3+x) = 4(2+x)$

Because the entire design of that process is to cancel the denominators, we know that conducting the process will do that for us. Accordingly, we can streamline the process by making that assumption, and simply multiplying each side by the other's denominator – essentially cross-multiplying each numerator by the opposing denominator:

$$\frac{3}{(2+x)} = \frac{4}{(3+x)}$$

The result is the same as before, just in fewer steps:

$3(3+x) = 4(2+x)$

We can then solve as usual:

$3 * 3 + 3x = 4 * 2 + 4x$ Eliminate parentheses

$9 + 3x = 8 + 4x$ Perform multiplication

$9 - 8 + 3x - 3x = 8 - 8 + 4x - 3x$ Subtract the same terms from both sides to isolate the variable

$1 = x$

Lazy Genius: Cross-multiplication is a helpful tool for reducing your workload, as long as you understand when it can be appropriately used – to use it, each side must be its own, single fraction with one denominator. If there are multiple terms on either side, you must first combine them to exist as one fraction per side before starting to cross multiply.

Drill – Simplifying Equations

Please simplify:

1. $4(3x + 2y - 18) + 16x - 3y + 14 =$

2. $(12 + x + 38)(81 - 4x - 79) =$

3. $5x^2 + 6x + 2z^2 + y^3 - 2x^2 + 2y^2 - 3z^2 =$

4. $3x^3 + 2x^2 - x^2y + xy^2 - 2x^3 =$

Solve for x:

5. $6x - 2 = 2x + 4$

6. $\dfrac{3}{x} = \dfrac{7}{(x + 12)}$

7. $3y + 17 = 5y - 17$

8. $-3(14 - 2x) = -6 - 2x$

Solving Equations

As we've discussed, equations can be solved by carrying out the same operation(s) on each side of the equation until a variable is isolated on its own. You can use the following operations as means to solve an equation:

$+$ $-$ $\cdot$ $\div$ $\sqrt{}$ $(\ )^n$

Addition   Subtraction   Multiplication   Division   Roots   Exponents

The key, again, is to be sure to perform the operation to each side of the equation, and not simply to any individual terms.

Example: $x = 3 - y$. *What is* x^2

In this case, to solve for x^2, we need to take the square root of the entire right side of the equation, and not simply square 3 and y individually: $x^2 = (3 - y)^2$ NOT $x = 3^2 - y^2$

Examples:

$$3x + 5 = 14$$
$$\underline{-5 \quad -5} \qquad \textit{subtract 5 from both sides}$$
$$\frac{3x}{3} = \frac{9}{3} \qquad \textit{divide both sides by 3}$$
$$x = 3$$

$$\frac{x}{2} = 4x - 7$$
$$\frac{2x}{2} = 2(4x - 7) \qquad \textit{multiply both sides by 2}$$
$$x = 8x - 14 \qquad \textit{subtract x from both sides}$$
$$\underline{-x = -x}$$
$$0 = 7x - 14$$
$$\underline{+14 = \quad + 14} \qquad \textit{add 14 to both sides}$$
$$\frac{14}{7} = \frac{7x}{7}$$
$$\qquad\qquad\qquad \textit{divide by the coefficient of 7}$$
$$2 = x$$

How Your Mind Works: A common mental mistake, and one upon which the GMAT writers thrive, is to see an opportunity to shortcut the math and jump on it – as seen above, squaring 3 and y individually would seem quick and easy. To avoid this trap when solving algebraic equations, put parentheses around each side of the equation to remind yourself that an operation you perform must apply to the entire side, and not just an individual term; in this way, the equation above would be: $x = (3 - y)$

Solving Equations Drill

Solve for x:

1. $5x - 2 = 2x + 13$

2. $\dfrac{3}{x} = \dfrac{9}{(x + 4)}$

3. $4 - 12x = 8x - 26$

4. $5x - 15 = 3(10 + x) - 5$

5. $2(3x - 7) + 4x = 8(4 + x) - 20$

6. $\dfrac{8}{x} = \dfrac{12}{(3x + 9)}$

Solutions – Simplifying and Solving Equations

1. Simplify $3x - y + 2x + 9y$
$5x + 8y$

2. Simplify $3x^2 + 4x + 5x^2 + 6x$
$8x^2 + 10x$

3. Simplify $x + y + z - x + y + z$
$2y + 2z$

Simplifying Equations

1. $4(3x + 2y - 18) + 16x - 3y + 14 =$
$28x + 5y - 58$

2. $(12 + x + 38)(81 - 4x - 79) =$

$100 - 198x - 4x^2$

3. $5x^2 + 6x + 2z^2 + y^3 - 2x^2 + 2y^2 - 3z^2 =$
$3x^2 + 6x + y^3 + 2y^2 - z^2$

4. $3x^3 + 2x^2 - x^2y + xy^2 - 2x^3 =$
$x^3 + 2x^2 - x^2y + xy^2$

5. $6x - 2 = 2x + 4$

$x = \dfrac{3}{2}$

6. $\dfrac{3}{x} = \dfrac{7}{(x + 12)}$
$x = 9$

7. $3y + 17 = 5y - 17$
$y = 17$

8. $-3(14 - 2x) = -6 - 2x$
$x = 4.5$

Solving Equations Drill

1. $5x - 2 = 2x + 13$
$x = 5$

2. $\dfrac{3}{x} = \dfrac{9}{(x + 4)}$
$x = 2$

3. $4 - 12x = 8x - 26$

$x = \dfrac{3}{2}$

4. $5x - 15 = 3(10 + x) - 5$
$x = 20$

5. $2(3x - 7) + 4x = 8(4 + x) - 20$
$x = 13$

6. $\dfrac{8}{x} = \dfrac{12}{(3x + 9)}$
$x = -6$

Multiple Variables and Multiple Equations

Some problems involve more than one variable. When solving a problem with N variables, you will most likely need N unique, linear equations in order to solve for them. Be sure, however, that the equations are unique; the following two equations are essentially the same, and would not permit you to solve for either variable:

$x + 5 = y$ $2x + 10 = 2y$

Because the second equation can be created simply by multiplying both sides of the first by 2, it does not add new information. In order to solve for either x or y in the first equation, you would need a second unique equation.

On the GMAT you will be required to solve equations with two unknowns. You are highly unlikely to encounter more than three unknowns and three equations. Nonetheless, the approach to equations with multiple unkowns is the same:

1.   Express one variable using the other variables in an equation.

2.   Plug this new expression into another of the given equations.

3.   Repeat until you solve one variable, and then substitute the variable with its value in the other equations.

Examples:

$x + y = 7$

$x - y = 1$ *(two equations and two unknowns, x and y)*

Express one variable using the other variables in an equation.
$x - y = 1 \rightarrow x = 1 + y$

Plug this new expression into another of the given equations.
$x + y = 7 \rightarrow (1 + y) + y = 7 \rightarrow 2y = 7 - 1 \rightarrow y = 3$

Repeat until you solve one variable, and then substitute the variable with its value in the

other equations.
$$x = 1 + y \to x = 1 + 3 \to x = 4$$

Alternative Approach

Add or subtract both sides of two or more equations to solve the equation directly. This is permissible because both sides are equal; you will be adding or subtracting the same amount to both sides.

$$x + y = 7$$

(two equations and two unknowns, x and y)

$$x - y = 1$$

Add both sides of the two equations together.
$$(x + y) + (x - y) = 7 + 1 \to 2x = 8 \to x = 4$$

In either equation, substitute one of the variables with its known value.
$$x + y = 7 \to 4 + y = 7 \to y = 3$$

Multiple Variables Drill

Solve for x and y:

1. $x + y = 10$ $x - y = 6$

2. $3x - y = 8$ $x = -5y$

3. $3x + 2y = 9$ $y = x + 2$

4. $3x + y = 8$ $x - 2y = -2$

5. $2y - 3x = 12$ $y + 2x = 10$

Solving For Multiple Variables

As we have seen, solving for multiple variables will most likely require you to have as many equations as variables. There are a few exceptions:

Definitions: Should one of the variables be limited by a definition such as "x must be a positive integer" or "y is a prime number", the pool of possible solutions may be narrowed to a point where you can solve with fewer equations.

Inequalities: Inequalities, such as $x < 5$, can also limit the pool of possibilities and allow you to solve for multiple variables with fewer solutions.

Example: *If x, y, and z are prime numbers such that $x<y<z$, and $x + y + z = 10$, what is the value of y?*

Solution: Because the definitions limit x, y, and z to prime numbers, we can determine that only one combination of prime numbers will add to 10: $2 + 3 + 5$. The next largest prime number is 7, and could not be combined with any two other prime numbers to produce a sum as low as 10. Accordingly, our options are limited to a point that we can determine that $x = 2$, $y = 3$, and $z = 5$, so the answer to this particular question is 3.

Outside of these exceptions, a good rule of thumb is that, when faced with more variables than equations, you should:

1) Search for more equations

OR

2) Consolidate your variables

The GMAT writers understand that examinees are under stress to act quickly, and have a tendency to miss key words that will allow them to find additional equations or eliminate or consolidate variables.

Example: *In preparation for a trip to New York, Xavier made two identical ATM withdrawals, and Yoni made one. Together, they withdrew exactly enough to each contribute $60 to the travel fund. How much money did Xavier withdraw on his first trip?*

We do know that $x_1 + x_2 + y = 120$, and that $x_1 + x_2 = 60$, but that still leaves us one equation short. Looking back, the word "identical" alerts us that Xavier's first withdrawal was the same as his second, and we know then that $x_1 = x_2$. The lesson? Words like "identical" and "the same" are easy to overlook, but will help us to create new equations or consolidate our variables in order to solve for multiple variables.

Absolute Value

Absolute Value, denoted by the symbol $|n|$, notes a value's "distance from zero".

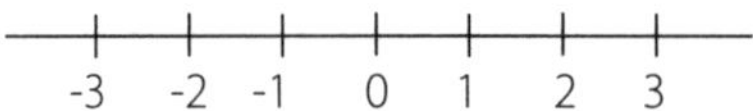

On the number line, 3 and -3 are equally far from 0 on each side. Therefore, they have the same absolute value.

When using absolute value in algebraic terms, it is important to note that there are two values for each absolute value – that is to say that, if a variable has an absolute value of, say, 5, the variable could be either 5 or -5, because each of those values is 5 places away from zero:

$|x| = 5 \rightarrow$ x could be 5 or -5, because $|-5| = 5$ and $|5| = 5$

Accordingly, any algebraic expression contained within the absolute value bars needs to be seen as two equations – one that results in the positive, absolute value, and the other which will result in its opposite:

$|x + 5| = 10 \rightarrow$

$x + 5 = 10$	OR	$x + 5 = -10$
$\underline{-5 = -5}$		$\underline{-5 = -5}$
$x = 5$		$x = -15$

$|2x - 3| = 7 \rightarrow$

$2x - 3 = 7$	OR	$2x - 3 = -7$
$\underline{+3 = +3}$		$\underline{+3 = +3}$
$2x = 10$		$2x = -4$
$x = 5$		$x = -2$

Absolute Value Drill

Solve for x:

1. $|15 - 3x| = 12$

2. $|5 - x| = 13$

3. $|x - 12| = 18$

4. $|3x + 2| = 11$

5. $|2x - 3| = 30 - x$

Solutions – Multiple Variables and Absolute Value

Multiple Variables

1. $x + y = 10$ $x - y = 6$
$x = 8; y = 2$

2. $3x - y = 8$ $x = -5y$
$x = \frac{5}{2}; y = -\frac{1}{2}$

3. $3x + 2y = 9$ $y = x + 2$
$x = 1; y = 3$

4. $3x + y = 8$ $x - 2y = -2$
$x = 2; y = 2$

5. $2y - 3x = 12$ $y + 2x = 10$
$x = \frac{8}{7}; y = \frac{54}{7}$

Absolute Value

1. $|15 - 3x| = 12$
$x = 1; x = 9$

2. $|5 - x| = 13$
$x = -8; x = 18$

3. $|x - 12| = 18$
$x = -6; x = 30$

4. $|3x + 2| = 11$
$x = -\frac{13}{3}; x = 3$

5. $|2x - 3| = 30 - x$

$x = -27; x = 11$

Inequalities

Inequalities are similar to normal algebraic equations, except that the equal sign is substituted with one the following symbols:

A	$\neq$	B	A is not equal to B
A	$>$	B	A is greater than B
A	$\geq$	B	A is greater or equal to B
A	$<$	B	A is less than B
A	$\leq$	B	A is less or equal to B

All the rules that apply to equations also apply to inequalities (i.e. whatever operation you apply to one side of an equation you have to apply to the other side). The only difference – but an important difference – with inequalities is that if you multiply or divide both sides by a negative number the inequality sign is flipped.

For a demonstration of why the sign must be flipped, consider the statement that:

"Two is greater than one" $\rightarrow 2 > 1$

If we were to multiply both by -1, we would produce the expression $\rightarrow -2 > -1$

We know the above to be incorrect; 2 is a larger value than 1, and so its negative value will carry it farther from 0 than will the same for 1. In order to account for this, we must flip the sign when multiplying or dividing by a negative:

$-2 < -1 \rightarrow$ this is correct; -2 is less than -1

Examples:

$8 > 3 \rightarrow (-1) \cdot 8 > (-1) \cdot 3 \rightarrow -8 < -3$

$2x + 10 \geq 4 \rightarrow 2x \geq 4 - 10 \rightarrow x \geq -3$

$3y - 3 < 5y + 7 \rightarrow 3y - 5y < 7 + 3 \rightarrow -2y < 10 \rightarrow \frac{-2y}{-2} < \frac{10}{-2} \rightarrow y > -5$

Multiple Inequalities

When an expression features "bracketed" inequalities – three quantities separated by two inequalities as seen below, you must treat each inequality as a different statement for the purposes of performing algebraic operations:

$2 < x + 2 < 4$

In the statement above, the algebra should be relatively straightforward – one would just need to subtract 2 from both sides to isolate x. However with three quantities, there is no way to perform the same operation for "both" sides, and so you should break each inequality apart and treat as two separate problems:

$$\begin{array}{lcl} 2 < x + 2 & \text{AND} & x + 2 < 4 \\ \underline{-2 \quad -2} & & \underline{-2 \ -2} \\ 0 < x & \text{AND} & x < 2 \end{array}$$

Then, you can take the findings from each statement and reform the brackets if you wish:

$0 < x < 2$

For another example:

$y - 2 < x < 2y + 1$

$$\begin{array}{lcl} y - 2 < x & \text{AND} & x < 2y + 1 \\ \underline{\quad +2 +2} & & \underline{-1 \ -1} \\ y < x+2 & \text{AND} & \dfrac{x-1}{2} < \dfrac{2y}{2} \\ & & \dfrac{(x-1)}{2} < y \end{array}$$

Add/subtract from each
The left side is solved
Divide the coefficient
The right side is solved

Again, you can reform the bracketing inequalities found above if you wish:

$x + 2 > y > \dfrac{(x-1)}{2}$

Inequalities Drill

Determine the value of x as specifically as possible by manipulating the inequality (or inequalities).

1. $12 + 3x > 15 + x$

2. $0 > x$ and $-\frac{1}{x} > 17$

3. $13 - 4x < 5 + 2x$

4. $12 + y > 4 - x$ and $12 - 3y > 9$

5. $14 - x < y < 2x - 1$

Solutions – Inequalities

1. $12 + 3x > 15 + x$

$x > \dfrac{3}{2}$

2. $0 > x$ and $-\dfrac{1}{x} > 17$

$-\dfrac{1}{17} < x < 0$

3. $13 - 4x < 5 + 2x$

$x > \dfrac{4}{3}$

4. $12 + y > 4 - x$ and $12 - 3y > 9$

$x > -8 - y;\ y < 1$

5. $14 - x < y < 2x - 1$

$x > 14 - y;\ x > \dfrac{(y + 1)}{2}$

Exponents

Exponent rules, and their combination with variables, will be tested rather frequently on the GMAT. Like many rules you will learn, it is a good idea to memorize them so that you have them handy when necessary; the list below will denote the rules you should know. With these and other rules, however, you should also note that rules must hold for all numbers, and can therefore be tested with small numbers if you are unsure of whether your memory is correct. As we demonstrate these rules, we will also show how they can be derived; you will likely find that understanding why a rule must hold true is the easiest way to ensure that you memorize it effectively.

Rule	Explanation
$(x \cdot y)^a = x^a \cdot y^a$	This rule applies the distributive property covered earlier; you can also attempt to prove it using smaller numbers: $(2 \cdot 3)^2 = 6^2 = 36$ OR $(2 \cdot 3)^2 = 2^2 \cdot 3^2 = 4 \cdot 9 = 36$
$\left(\dfrac{x}{y}\right)^a = \dfrac{x^a}{y^a}$	Similar to above; the distributive property dictates that the exponent, a, will apply to all terms within the parentheses.
$x^a \cdot x^b = x^{a+b}$	Try this with small numbers representing the exponents, such as $a = 2$ and $b = 3$: $x^2 \cdot x^3 = (x \cdot x) \cdot (x \cdot x \cdot x)$ or x^5.
$(x^a)^b = x^{ab}$	Similar to above, try using $a = 2$ and $b = 3$: $(x^2)^3 = (x \cdot x)(x \cdot x)(x \cdot x) = x^6$
$x^{-a} = \dfrac{1}{x^a}$ $\dfrac{1}{y^{-b}} = y^b$	The two statements to the left are inverses of each other; negative exponents should be seen as signifying reciprocals.
$\dfrac{x^a}{x^b} = x^{a-b}$	An intermediate step will prove this to be true; because the denominator can be expressed as the numerator to the negative exponent, $\dfrac{x^a}{x^b} = x^a \cdot x^{-b} = x^{a-b}$
$x^0 = 1$	This one may seem counterintuitive, but can be proven using the items noted above. We can express the statement $\dfrac{x^2}{x^2}$ in fraction form, or use the negative-exponent property to express it as $x^2 \cdot x^{-2}$. In the latter, we would add the exponents to create x^0; in the former, it is clear that the same value, when divided by itself, will produce 1. Accordingly, $x^0 = 1$.

Exponent Drill

$8^2 \cdot 8^3 =$

$(4 \cdot 7)^4 =$

$(5^3)^7 =$

$(\frac{2}{5})^3 =$

$\frac{7^{11}}{7^5} =$

$5^{-2} =$

$3/7^{-3} =$

$11^0 =$

$8^1 =$

Exponent Drill Solutions

$8^2 \cdot 8^3 =$	$x^a \cdot x^b = x^{a+b}$	$8^2 \cdot 8^3 = 8^{2+3} = 8^5$
$(4 \cdot 7)^4 =$	$(xy)^a = x^a \cdot y^a$	$(4 \cdot 7)^4 = 4^4 \cdot 7^4$
$(5^3)^7 =$	$(x^a)^b = x^{ab}$	$(5^3)^7 = 5^{3 \cdot 7} = 5^{21}$
$(\frac{2}{5})^3 =$	$(\frac{x}{y})^a = \frac{x^a}{y^a}$	$(\frac{2}{5})^3 = \frac{2^3}{5^3}$
$\frac{7^{11}}{7^5} =$	$\frac{x^a}{x^b} = x^{a-b}$	$\frac{7^{11}}{7^5} = 7^{11-5} = 7^6$
$5^{-2} =$	$x^{-a} = \frac{1}{x^a}$	$5^{-2} = \frac{1}{5^2}$
$3/7^{-3} =$	$\frac{1}{y^{-b}} = y^b$	$\frac{3}{7^{-3}} = 3 \cdot 7^3$
$11^0 =$	$x^0 = 1$	$11^0 = 1$
$8^1 =$	$x^1 = x$	$8^1 = 8$

Exponentials Drill

Simplify the following equations:

1. $4 \cdot x^3 \cdot 5x \cdot x^2y \cdot 5y$

2. $\dfrac{48\, z^4 y^{-3}}{12zy^2}$

3. $\dfrac{72x^3 y^4 z}{(2xyz^2)^3}$

4. $\dfrac{14x^2 x^{-3} y^4}{7x^{-4} y^{-1}}$

5. $(6x \cdot 2y^3)^2$

6. $\dfrac{2^3 \cdot 6^2}{18 \cdot 16^{\frac{1}{2}}}$

7. $\dfrac{15^3 \cdot 8}{2^2 \cdot 6^3}$

Solutions - Exponentials

1. $4 \cdot x^3 \cdot 5x \cdot x^2 y \cdot 5y = 100x^6 y^2$

2. $\dfrac{48\, z^4 y^3}{12 z y^2} = \dfrac{4z^3}{y^5}$

3. $\dfrac{72 x^3 y^4 z}{(2xyz^2)^3} = \dfrac{9y}{z^5}$

4. $\dfrac{14 x^2 x^{-3} y^4}{7 x^{-4} y^{-1}} = 2x^3 y^5$

5. $(6x \cdot 2y^3)^2 = 144 x^2 y^6$

6. $\dfrac{2^3 \cdot 6^2}{18 \cdot 16^{\frac{1}{2}}} = 4$

7. $\dfrac{15^3 \cdot 8}{2^2 \cdot 6^3} = 31.25$

Roots

While exponents ask us to multiply a value by itself a number of times, roots do exactly the opposite – roots, instead, ask "which number multiplied by itself (a certain number of times) will produce this value?" The most common root, the square root, asks "which number, squared, will produce this value?" Accordingly, the square root of 16 asks for a number that, when squared, will produce 16 – that number is 4, as we see in the first example below. By mathematical convention (which the GMAT follows to the letter), the radical sign, $\sqrt{\ }$, represents only the positive square root.

Examples:

If $x^2 = 16$, then $x = 4$ or -4 BUT $\sqrt{16} = 4$ only

$\sqrt{\dfrac{4}{25}} = \dfrac{2}{5}$ $\qquad$ *because* $\qquad$ $\left(\dfrac{2}{5}\right)^2 = \dfrac{4}{25}$

$\sqrt{16 \cdot 36} = 4 \cdot 6$ $\qquad$ *because* $\qquad$ $(4 \cdot 6)^2 = 4^2 \cdot 6^2 = 16 \cdot 36$

$\sqrt{x^{12}} = x^6$ $\qquad$ *because* $\qquad$ $(x^6)^2 = x^{6 \cdot 2} = x^{12}$

$(\sqrt{x})^2 = x$ $\qquad$ *and* $\qquad$ $\sqrt{x^2} = |x|$

Note
While there are many roots, which we will cover in the coming pages, the standard is the square root, and the radical sign, $\sqrt{\ }$, with no other notations, represents the square root.

Roots Are Fractional Exponents

As mentioned above, roots and exponents are closely linked, as roots represent a logical inverse of exponents. In fact, roots can be represented mathematically as exponents, allowing us to employ the exponent rules we've learned in the previous pages as methods to solve problems using roots. In doing so, the square root of 16 could be represented exponentially:

$\sqrt{16} = 16^{\frac{1}{2}} \rightarrow$ the numerator of the exponent will remain an exponent (in this case, 16-to-the-first power), but the denominator represents the root (in this case, the square root).

Essentially, this statement is asking for "the square root of 16 to the first power".

This same statement above can be rewritten to further demonstrate the point. Because 16 is equal to both 4^2 and 2^4, we can express its root as functions of each number:

$$\sqrt{16} = \sqrt{4^2} = 4^{\frac{2}{2}} = 4^1$$
$$\sqrt{16} = \sqrt{2^4} = 2^{\frac{4}{2}} = 2^2 = 4$$

Definitions for Factorizing Roots

Roots, because they are essentially types of exponents, will follow the same rules as exponents do:

$$\sqrt{\frac{a}{b}} = \frac{\sqrt{a}}{\sqrt{b}}$$

$$\sqrt{a \cdot b} = \sqrt{a} \cdot \sqrt{b}$$

Examples:

$$\sqrt{\frac{1}{16}} = \frac{\sqrt{1}}{\sqrt{16}} = \frac{1}{4}$$

$$\sqrt{72} = \sqrt{36 \cdot 2} = \sqrt{36} \cdot \sqrt{2} = 6\sqrt{2}$$

$$\sqrt{\frac{7}{16}} = \frac{\sqrt{7}}{\sqrt{16}} = \frac{\sqrt{7}}{4}$$

$$\sqrt{3} \cdot \sqrt{12} = \sqrt{3 \cdot 12} = \sqrt{36} = 6$$

Addition and Subtraction

Add and subtract roots as you would any variable:

$$x + x + x + x = 4x \qquad \sqrt{2} + \sqrt{2} + \sqrt{2} + \sqrt{2} = 4\sqrt{2} \quad (4\sqrt{2} \text{ is the same as } 4 \cdot \sqrt{2})$$

As with variables, you can only combine like roots.

$$x + x + y = 2x + y \quad \sqrt{2} + \sqrt{2} + \sqrt{8} = 2\sqrt{2} + \sqrt{8}$$

But roots have one property that makes them unique when it comes to adding and subtracting – because we can factor them, in many cases we know more about roots than we would about a variable. Remember that, based on the rules of factoring exponents:

$$\sqrt{8} = \sqrt{4 \cdot 2} = \sqrt{4}\,\sqrt{2}$$

As a result, we can break that term down further:

$\sqrt{4}\,\sqrt{2} = 2\sqrt{2}$, so the initial equation $2\sqrt{2} + \sqrt{8} = 2\sqrt{2} + 2\sqrt{2} = 4\sqrt{2}$

Other Roots

As noted previously, the square root $\sqrt{x}$ is the same as $\sqrt[2]{x}$. Because the square root is so common, the 2 preceding the radical sign is simply considered redundant.

Any value for a in the root $\sqrt[a]{x}$ is possible. This simply means that we are looking for the number that when raised to the power of a equals x.

Roots with odd exponents (3, 5, 7, 9. etc.) may have negative values for x.

> *Facts & Formulas:* $\sqrt[a]{x}$ can be rewritten as $x^{\frac{1}{a}}$

Examples:

$\sqrt[3]{-64} = -4\ because\ -4 \cdot -4 \cdot -4 = -64$

$\left(\sqrt[4]{25}\right)^2 = (25^{1/4})^2 = 25^{(1/4)\cdot2} = 25^{2/4} = 25^{1/2} = \sqrt{25}$

Roots on the GMAT

An important note pertaining to the GMAT: You are responsible for knowing that there is a positive and negative root for each squared term. For example:

> *GMAT Insider:* Problem Solving questions will tend to use the radical sign, as you will typically be asked to solve for a particular value; Data Sufficiency questions will often provide the square as part of an equation, forcing you to remember that there are, indeed, two roots for any square.

If $x^2 = 16$, x could equal 4 or -4

However, when the radical sign, $\sqrt{\ }$, is provided, the equation is asking simply for the principal square root, or the positive root. Therefore:

$$\sqrt{16} = 4$$

On the GMAT, this is primarily done to allow you to use roots within other calculations as you saw on the previous page.

Roots Drill

Solve.

1. $2\sqrt{5} + 3\sqrt{5} + \sqrt{5} =$

2. $\sqrt{\dfrac{9}{16}} =$

3. $\sqrt{z^8} =$

4. $\dfrac{(\sqrt{3} - 6)}{\sqrt{3}} =$

5. $\sqrt{(12 \cdot 3 \cdot 8)} =$

6. $\dfrac{3\sqrt{3} + 2}{\sqrt{3}} =$

7. $3\sqrt{2} + 2\sqrt{8} + \sqrt{32} =$

Solutions - Roots Drill

1. $2\sqrt{5} + 3\sqrt{5} + \sqrt{5} = 6\sqrt{5}$

2. $\sqrt{\dfrac{9}{16}} = \dfrac{3}{4}$

3. $\sqrt{z^8} = z^4$

4. $\dfrac{(\sqrt{3}-6)}{\sqrt{3}} \cdot \dfrac{\sqrt{3}}{\sqrt{3}} = \dfrac{\sqrt{3}(\sqrt{3}-6)}{3} = \dfrac{3-6\sqrt{3}}{3} = \dfrac{3-6\sqrt{3}}{3} = 1 - 2\sqrt{3}$

5. $\sqrt{(12 \cdot 3 \cdot 8)} = 12\sqrt{2}$

6. $\dfrac{3\sqrt{3}+2}{\sqrt{3}} \cdot \dfrac{\sqrt{3}}{\sqrt{3}} = \dfrac{\sqrt{3}(3\sqrt{3}+2)}{3} = \dfrac{9+2\sqrt{3}}{3} = 3 + \dfrac{2\sqrt{3}}{3}$

7. $3\sqrt{2} + 2\sqrt{8} + \sqrt{32} = 11\sqrt{2}$

Multiple Solutions

Sometimes an algebraic equation has more than one solution. Consider the equation:

$$x(x - 9)(x^2 - 9)(x^2 + 9) = 0$$

There are four solutions to this: $x = 0$, $x = 9$, $x = 3$, and $x = -3$.

Because on the GMAT, x^2 cannot be negative[1] , $(x^2 + 9)$ cannot equal zero.

Note
$x^2 - 9 = 0$ has two solutions, because a negative number squared becomes positive. Both 3 and -3 would make this equation true.

As seen above, equations that will require multiple solutions – most often on the GMAT, such equations will include squares – are easiest solved when factored into a number of terms for which the product is zero. Accordingly, each term, when set equal to zero, will provide a solution to the equation.

Three Common Equations

In a moment, we will demonstrate how to factor equations, but recognizing the below equations will save you time:

1. $(x + y)^2 = (x + y)(x + y) = x^2 + 2xy + y^2$

Example: $x^2 + 8x + 16 = 0 \rightarrow (x + 4)^2 = 0$, and $x = -4$

2. $(x - y)^2 = (x - y)(x - y) = x^2 - 2xy + y^2$

Example: $x^2 - 18x + 81 = 0 \rightarrow (x - 9)^2 = 0$, and $x = 9$

3. $(x + y)(x - y) = x^2 - y^2$ Also known as the "difference of squares"

Example: $x^2 - 64 = 0 \rightarrow (x + 8)(x - 8) = 0$, and $x = 8$ or -8

Lazy Genius: The third equation, of the "difference of squares" variety, often presents an easy opportunity to simplify more complex equations. Learn to recognize and apply it, as it will save significant time when employed.

[1] There is actually a solution, but it requires the use of imaginary numbers. Only real numbers are covered on the GMAT.

Quadratic Equations, FOIL, and Factoring

In addition to the squares and difference-of-squares equations presented on the previous page, you may see a variety of quadratic equations presented on the GMAT. Quadratic equations come in the form:

$$ax^2 + bx + c = 0$$

where a and b represent coefficients. As discussed earlier, the best way to solve equations with multiple solutions is to express them as a series of terms multiplying to a product of 0. In this case, each individual term, when set equal to 0, represents a solution to the equation:

$$(x + y)(x + z) = 0$$

As you may remember (fondly) from high school, you can multiply out expressions of the latter variety to eliminate the parentheses, using the FOIL method. FOIL is an easy way to remember to distribute the multiplication in such an expression across all terms:

First		**Outside**		**Inside**		**Last**
$x \cdot x$	+	$x \cdot z$	+	$x \cdot y$	+	$y \cdot z$

In this approach, you will multiply the first terms in each quantity, then the outside terms, then the inside terms, then the last terms, adding each product together.

Examples:

$(x + 4)(x-2)$

First		*Outside*		*Inside*		*Last*
$x \cdot x$	+	$x \cdot (-2)$	+	$x \cdot 4$	+	$4 \cdot (-2)$

$$x^2 - 2x + 4x - 8 = x^2 + 2x - 8$$

$(x + 7)(x + 2)$

First		*Outside*		*Inside*		*Last*
$x \cdot x$	+	$x \cdot 2$	+	$x \cdot 7$	+	$7 \cdot 2$

$$x^2 + 9x + 14$$

Factoring

Because, when solving for quadratic equations, your goal will be to take the equations from the expanded format and express them instead as a product of terms equaling zero, you will want to employ the reverse of the FOIL method. Using the same principles, you will be able to take most quadratics on the GMAT and convert them to products.

Consider the example from the previous page:

$x^2 + 2x - 8$

Should we want to convert it back to its "pre-FOIL" form, which will allow us to solve for its two solutions, we can use what we know about the FOIL method to do so:

The first term in the quadratic above will be created by the first terms multiplied, and the last terms will be created by the last terms, leaving the middle term to be formed by the outside and inside terms. Visually, we will see:

First	Outside/Inside	Last
x^2	$+ 2x$	$- 8$

Accordingly, the terms of our solution will need to be constructed to produce the above. In the expression below:

$(x + a)(x + b)$

The Outside and Inside terms need to create 2x, and the Last terms need to create -8. Because the Outside and Inside terms each contain one x, we can simplify this search:

$ab \rightarrow$ must equal -8
$a + b \rightarrow$ must equal 2

Accordingly, our strategy should be to:

1) Determine the possible factors of the Last term (ab): $1 \cdot 8$; $2 \cdot 4$

2) Find a pair that adds to the Outside/Inside term (a + b): $4 + -2$

3) Enter these terms within the parentheses, and set each term equal to zero:

$(x + 4)(x - 2) = 0$

$x = -4$ or 2

In summary, when factoring quadratic equations to the form $(x + a)(x + b)$, the a and b terms must multiply to the last number, and add to the middle coefficient: $a^2 + (a + b)x + ab$

Factoring Drill

Solve for x, y, or z by factoring the quadratic equation.

1. $x^2 - 6x + 9 = 0$

2. $x^2 - 9x + 14 = 0$

3. $x^2 + 7x - 60 = 0$

4. $z^2 + 18z + 77 = 0$

5. $y^2 + y - 110 = 0$

6. $y^2 - y - 56 = 0$

7. $x^2 + 12x + 36 = 0$

8. $y^2 - 11y - 42 = 0$

9. $z^2 + 14y + 45 = 0$

Solutions - Factoring Drill

1. $x^2 - 6x + 9 = 0$
     $x = 3$

2. $x^2 - 9x + 14 = 0$
     $x = 2; x = 7$

3. $x^2 + 7x - 60 = 0$
     $x = -12; x = 5$

4. $z^2 + 18z + 77 = 0$
     $z = -11; z = -7$

5. $y^2 + y - 110 = 0$
     $y = -11; y = 10$

6. $y^2 - y - 56 = 0$
     $y = -7; y = 8$

7. $x^2 + 12x + 36 = 0$
     $x = -6$

8. $y^2 - 11y - 42 = 0$
     $y = -3; y = 14$

9. $z^2 + 14y + 45 = 0$
     $z = -9; z = -5$

Conversions

A common questioning device that the GMAT uses to add difficulty is the requirement that an answer be given in different units than you may have used for the calculations. For example, if you determine that it took a factory 3 hours to produce 100 vehicles, the exam might ask for that answer to be given in minutes, and you would need to convert hours to minutes.

Rest assured, you are specifically responsible for very few conversion factors – the exam will not require you to convert pints to gallons, Fahrenheit to Celsius, or bushels to pecks – but you will need to effectively perform the conversions that the test does require. This may not be as easy as it sounds. Consider the following:

Example of a Common Conversion Error:

A commuter makes the trip from Los Angeles to Newport Beach at an average rate of 60 miles per hour. What is her speed in miles per second?

Examinees are often confused as to how to convert hours to seconds, and will decide whether to multiply or divide the 60 seconds per minute and 60 minutes per hour that they know will need to be handled. The following is an example of such a conversion gone wrong:

$$60\frac{miles}{hour} \cdot 60\frac{minutes}{hour} \cdot 60\frac{seconds}{minute} = 216{,}000\frac{miles}{second}$$

This mistake is more common than you would think, and provides a drastically incorrect answer – 60 miles per hour does not convert to be faster than the speed of light!

Using Conversion Factors

To avoid these errors, we can use our knowledge of algebra and of fractions to set up conversion equations that will always produce the correct answer in the correct units. Units will factor the same way that numbers and variables do:

$$\frac{60\ miles}{1\ \cancel{hour}} \cdot \frac{1\ \cancel{hour}}{60\ \cancel{minutes}} \cdot \frac{1\ \cancel{minute}}{60\ seconds} = \frac{1\ mile}{60\ seconds}$$

Step One: Determine which units need to be eliminated; in this case, hours do not appear in the final answer, and should be eliminated first.

Step Two: Construct a fraction using a conversion ratio that will eliminate the desired units; in this case, 60 minutes : 1 hour is the appropriate ratio, with 1 hour appearing in the numerator to eliminate the unit "hours" in the denominator.

Step Three: Repeat the process as necessary until the desired units appear; in this case, the new denominator, "minutes", must still be eliminated, and we can use the ratio 1 minute : 60 seconds to finish the conversion to miles per second.

Step Four: Perform the mathematical calculations; the result will be expressed in the proper units due to the conversion process.

Conversions Drill

Other than conversions with time (seconds, minutes, hours, days, etc.) and basic metric calculations (kilo, centi, milli, etc.), any conversions that you need will be provided, as seen below.

1. What is 254 centimeters expressed in inches? (1 inch = 2.54 centimeters)

2. What is a furlong ($\frac{1}{8}$ mile) expressed in inches? (5,280 feet = 1 mile; 1 foot = 12 inches)

3. How fast is 60 miles per hour in feet per second (5,280 feet = 1 mile)

4. What is the flow rate of 270 $\frac{\text{gallons}}{\text{hour}}$ expressed in pints per minute?
(1 quart = 2 pints; 1 gallon = 4 quarts)

Word Problems

A large percentage of GMAT questions will come in the form of word problems, in which you will need to construct appropriate equations before performing algebra and/or arithmetic. Often, examinees miss these questions simply because they incorrectly construct mathematical expressions in their haste to apply the quantitative concepts we have covered in the preceding pages. In order to efficiently and accurately construct appropriate expressions, you should plan to follow these steps when approaching word problems:

1)   Actively read the problem. As you read, determine what your known quantities are, and for what you will be asked to solve.

2)   Identify and define unknowns. When you find an unknown quantity, assign it a variable, and keep track of each individual variable. Often, questions will have multiple prices, rates, distances, etc., or force you to assign variables to several items that each begin with the same letter (a problem that begins with Alex, Becky, and Charles will be more difficult simply if the writers change the names to John, Jenny, and Jose). Use subscripts or assign different variables to avoid making errors.

3)   Express relationships mathematically. Construct equations and inequalities using the "language of mathematics" to convert from words to mathematical expressions:

$=$	$\rightarrow$	Is, was, will be, the same as, equal
$>$	$\rightarrow$	Greater than, more than
$<$	$\rightarrow$	Less than, smaller than
$+$	$\rightarrow$	Plus, and, added, combined, sum, greater than, more than
$-$	$\rightarrow$	Minus, less, subtracted, reduced, decreases, less than
$\cdot$	$\rightarrow$	Times, product, multiplied, doubled, tripled, of
$\div$	$\rightarrow$	Per, out of, divided, over

Note: The expressions "greater than", "more than" and "less than" can represent either inequalities or addition/subtraction. Remember that inequalities can take the place of equations; if those terms are used as part of an equation ("John's age is 5 years greater than Bryan's" – the word "is" sets up an equation), the expression will denote addition or subtraction. If no equation is provided, it will likely denote an inequality.

Examples:

1. Sidney's age is 5 years greater than Billy's.

First, assign variables. In this case, s for Sidney's age and b for Billy's seem to be apt. Then, express mathematically. Using our variables:

s is 5 greater than b
$s = 5 + b$

2. The price of a new car is 20% more than the wholesale cost to the dealer.

First, assign variables. Here we could use p for price and c for cost. Then, express mathematically:

p is 20% more than c
$p = 20/100 \ (c) + c$

Remember, with percentages, that the percent (20/100) must be taken of a value; in this case, the percentage pertains to the cost, as the equation is expressing the value of the price in terms of the cost.

3. Vandalay Industries' 2004 earnings were 150,000 less than twice its 2000 total.

Again, assign variables first. Here, the same initial letter would need to be used (v for Vandalay or e for earnings), so we can either use subscripts (V2004 and V2000) or assign unique variables (x = 2004 earnings and y = 2000 earnings). If we choose the latter, it is important to track which variable corresponds to which quantity. Then, express mathematically:

Vandalay's 2004 earnings **were** 150,000 less than **twice** its 2000 total.
$V_{2004} = 150,000$ less than $2(V_{2000})$

"Less than" can be tricky, as it signifies subtraction, but the value to be subtracted precedes the initial value. The statement above is saying that the 2004 earnings were almost twice as much as the 2000 earnings, just 150,000 less. Accordingly, the expression would be:

$V_{2004} = 2(V_{2000}) - 150,000$

Drill – Mathematically Speaking

In this drill, construct the following statements in mathematical terms; you will use the results later to solve full problems.

1. In a weight lifting competition, the total weight of Brian's two lifts was 650 pounds.

2. The weight of Brian's second lift was 150 pounds greater than that of his first.

3. An apple costs twice as much as a banana.

4. Josh purchased 15 apples and 12 bananas for a total of $21.

5. Sarah has six more dollars than does Priya.

6. If Priya were to double her money, she would have $30.

7. John is twice as old as Megan was four years ago.

8. In five years, Megan will be 30.

9. In five years, Dennis will be three times as old as Janet is then.

10. In five years, Janet will be 15.

Word Problems Drill

Using your equations from the previous page, answer the following questions:

1. In a weightlifting competition, the total weight of Brian's two lifts was 650 pounds. If his second lift was 150 pounds greater than his first lift, how heavy was his first lift?

2. Josh purchased 15 apples and 12 bananas for a total of $21. If an apple costs twice as much as a banana, what is the price of a banana?

3. Sarah has six more dollars than does Priya. If Priya doubles her money, she will have $30. How much money does Sarah have?

4. John is twice as old as Megan was four years ago. If, in 5 years, Megan will be 30, how old is John today?

5. In five years, Dennis will be three times as old as Janet is then. If Janet will be 15 in 5 years, how old is Dennis today?

Please answer the following questions:

6. If Rishi traveled 135 miles in 15 hours, what was his speed in miles per hour?

7. Mario saved more than $30 when buying his TV at a 15% discount. What is the least expensive price that the TV could have cost before the discount?

8. What did Glencoe Industries earn in the second quarter if it increased its $250,000 earnings by 40%?

9. What was the original price of a sweater if, after a 25% discount, it cost $60?

Solutions – Conversions

1. What is 254 centimeters expressed in inches? (1 inch = 2.54 centimeters)

254 cm · 1 inch/2.54 cm = 100 inches

2. What is a furlong (1/8 mile) expressed in inches? (5280 feet = 1 mile; 1 foot = 12 inches)

1 furlong · 1 mile/8 furlongs · 5280 feet/1 mile · 12 inches/1 foot = 7,920 inches

3. How fast is 60 miles per hour in feet per second (5280 feet = 1 mile)

60 miles/1 hour · 5280 feet/1 mile · 1 hour/60 minute · 1 minute/60 seconds = 88 feet/second

4. What is the flow rate of 270 gallons/hour expressed in pints per minute? (1 quart = 2 pints; 1 gallon = 4 quarts)

270 gallons/1 hour · 4 quarts/1 gallon · 2 pints/1 quart · 1 hour/60 minutes = 36 pints/minute

Solutions – Mathematically Speaking

1. In a weight lifting competition, the total weight of Brian's two lifts was 650 pounds.
First lift + second lift = 650
$x + y = 650$

2. The weight of Brian's second lift was 150 pounds greater than that of his first.
Second lift = 150 + first lift
$y = 150 + x$

3. An apple costs twice as much as a banana.
The cost of an apple is twice that of a banana
$a = 2b$

4. Josh purchased 15 apples and 12 bananas for a total of $21.
15 · cost of an apple + 12 · cost of a banana totals $21
$15a + 12b = 21$

5. Sarah has six more dollars than does Priya.
Sarah's total is 6 more than Priya's
$s = 6 + p$

6. If Priya were to double her money, she would have $30.
Twice Priya's amount is equal to $30
$2p = 30$

7. John is twice as old as Megan was four years ago.
$j = 2(m-4)$

8. In five years, Megan will be 30.
$m + 5 = 30$

9. In five years, Dennis will be three times as old as Janet is then.
Dennis' age in five years is equal to three times Janet's age in five years
$d + 5 = 3(j+5)$

10. In five years, Janet will be 15.
$j + 5 = 15$

Solutions - Word Problems

1. In a weightlifting competition, the total weight of Brian's two lifts was 650 pounds. If his second lift was 150 pounds greater than his first lift, how heavy was his first lift?

From the previous exercise, we know that our two equations are:

$$x + y = 650 \qquad\qquad y = 150 + x$$
We can substitute the equation on the right into the one on the left, expressing y in terms of x, and receive:
$$x + (150 + x) = 650$$
$$2x + 150 = 650$$
$$2x = 500$$
$x = 250$ pounds $\rightarrow$ because x represents "the first lift", we are finished.

2. Josh purchased 15 apples and 12 bananas for a total of $21. If an apple costs twice as much as a banana, what is the price of a banana?

From the previous exercise, we know that our two equations are:

$$a = 2b \qquad\qquad 15a + 12b = 21$$
We can substitute the equation on the left into the one on the right, expressing a in terms of b:
$$15(2b) + 12b = 21$$
$$30b + 12b = 21$$
$$42b = 21$$
$b = \$0.50 \rightarrow$ a banana costs $0.50

3. Sarah has six more dollars than does Priya. If Priya doubles her money, she will have $30. How much money does Sarah have?

From the previous exercise, we know that our two equations are:

$$s = 6 + p \qquad\qquad 2p = 30$$
Solving for the equation on the right by dividing by 2 to isolate p, we find that $p = 15$. Plugging that back into the equation on the left, we find that $s = 6 + 15 = 21$. Accordingly, Sarah has $21.

4. John is twice as old as Megan was four years ago. If, in 5 years, Megan will be 30, how old is John today?

From the previous exercise, we know that our equations are:
$$j = 2(m - 4) \qquad\qquad m + 5 = 30$$
Solving for the equation on the right, we find that $m = 25$. Plugging that into the equation on the left, we find that $j = 2(25 - 4) = 42$. John is 42 years old.

5. In five years, Dennis will be three times as old as Janet is then. If Janet will be 15 in 5 years, how old is Dennis today?

From the previous exercise, we know that our two equations are:

$d + 5 = 3(j + 5)$ $\qquad\qquad$ $j + 5 = 15$

Here, we can simply substitute the equation on the right for $j + 5$ into its place on the left, leaving us with:

$d + 5 = 3(15)$

$d + 5 = 45$

$d = 40 \rightarrow$ Dennis is 40 years old.

6. If Rishi traveled 135 miles in 15 hours, what was his speed in miles per hour?

Mathematically speaking, we know that Rishi's speed should be in miles per hour, or miles divided by hours. Accordingly we can set up the equation as:

Rate = miles/hour = 135 miles/15 hours = 9 miles per hour

7. Mario saved more than $30 when buying his TV at a 15% discount. What is the least expensive price that the TV could have cost before the discount?

Mario's savings, 15% off of the retail price, are more than $30. We can write this mathematically as:

15% of Retail > 30

$\dfrac{15}{100} R > 30$

$\dfrac{3}{20} R > 30$

$R > \dfrac{20}{3} \cdot 30$

$R > 200$

8. What did Glencoe Industries earn in the second quarter if it increased its $250,000 earnings by 40%?

Glencoe's earnings of $250,000 increased by 40% (of the original number)

$250{,}000 + \left(\dfrac{40}{100}\right)250{,}000$

$250{,}000 + \left(\dfrac{2}{5}\right)250{,}000$

$350,000 is the new total

9. What was the original price of a sweater if, after a 25% discount, it cost $60?

The sweater's retail price, minus 25% off (of itself) was $60

$$R - \frac{25}{100} R = 60$$

$$\frac{75}{100} R = 60$$

$$\frac{3}{4} R = 60$$

$$R = \frac{4}{360}$$

$R = 80 \rightarrow$ The shirt initially cost $80.

Lines and Angles

When we refer to "lines," we are describing straight lines that never alter direction.

Two lines that intersect form four angles, with two pairs of angles being identical on opposite sides of the intersection. The sum of the two angles on one side of a line always is 180°.

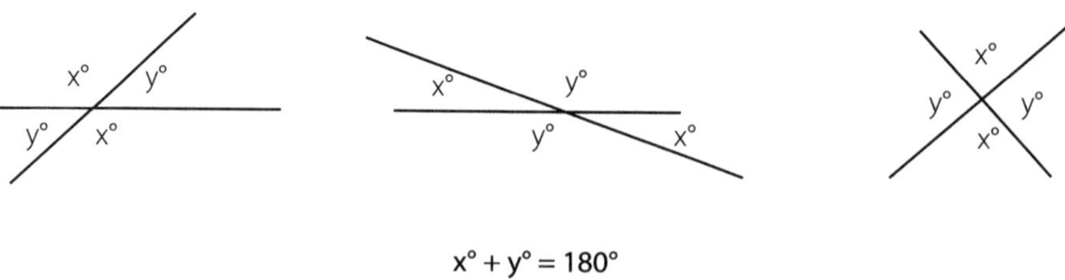

$$x° + y° = 180°$$

Parallel lines on a two-dimensional plane will never intersect.

Two **perpendicular lines** are at 90° to each other.

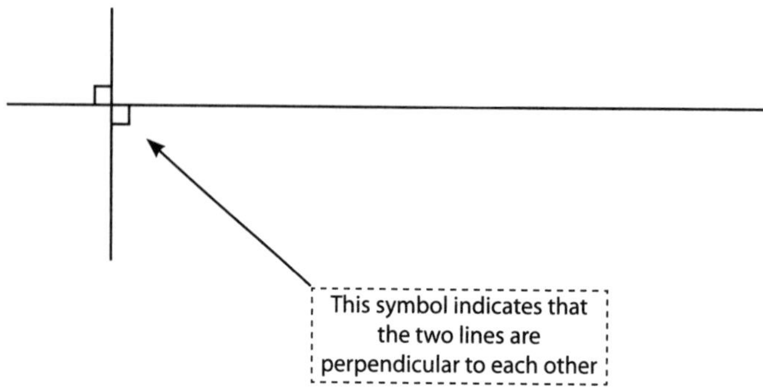

Example:

Fill in the missing angles.

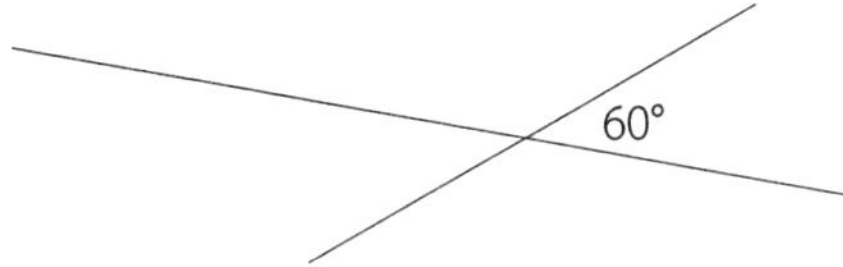

Step 1. Two angles on the same side of a line add up to 180° → 180 - 60 = 120

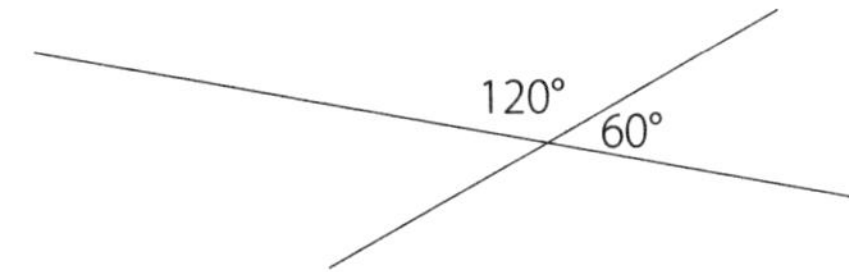

Step 2. Two pairs of angles are identical on opposite sides of the intersection.

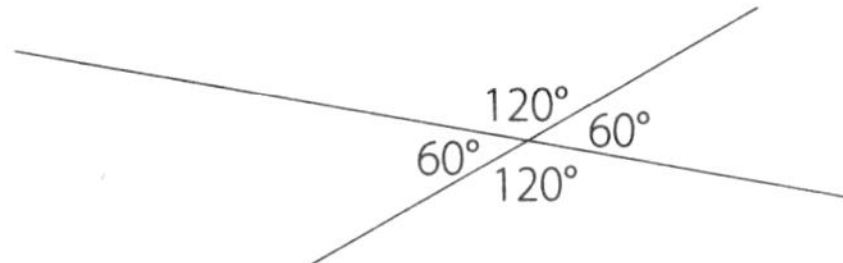

When two parallel lines are intersected by a third line, two sets of 4 identical angles are created:

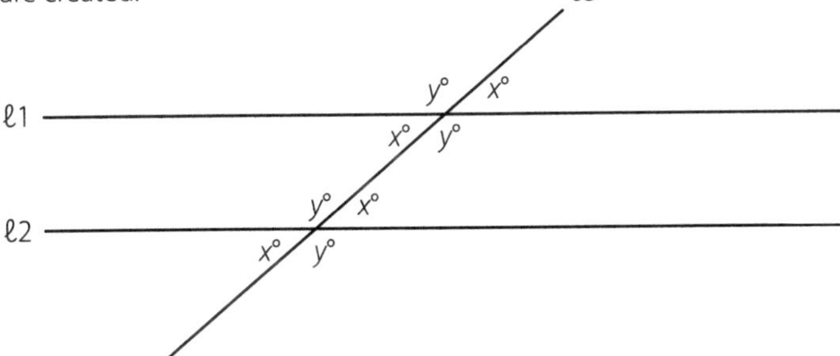

$\ell1$ is parallel to $\ell2$

While most students are comfortable with the concepts relating to lines and angles, they frequently forget to apply these rules on complex problems. Consider the following figure from a problem in the Geometry book:

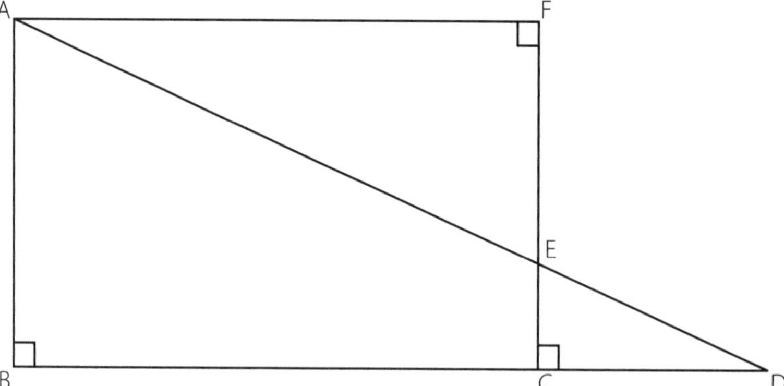

Note that angle CED is equal to angle AEF because of intersecting lines , and that angle CDE equals angle EAF because of parallel lines intersected by a straight line. It is very easy to overlook these facts and instead focus on other rules relating to triangles and quadrilaterals.

Lines and Angles Drill

Use the figure below to answer the following questions:

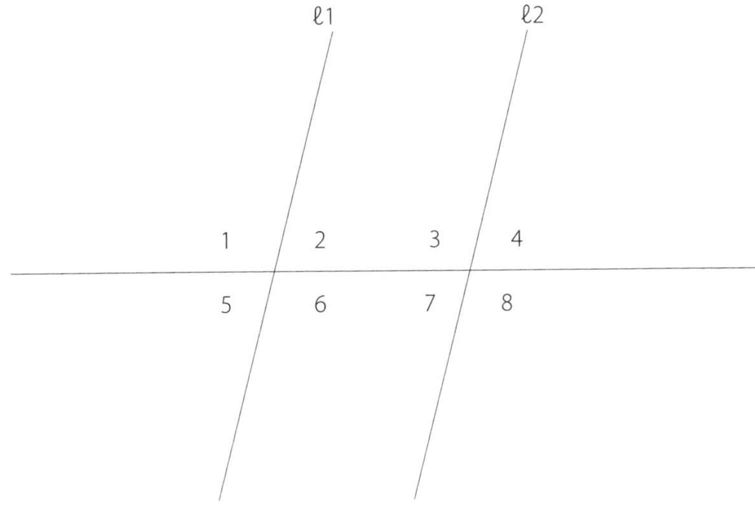

1. If the measure of angle 2 is 77°, what is the measure of angle 5?

2. If the measure of angle 2 is 77°, what is the measure of angle 1?

3. What is the sum of the measures of angles 1, 2, 5, and 6?

4. If ℓl and ℓ2 are parallel and the measure of angle 8 is 104°, what is the measure of angle 6?

5. If the measure of angle 1 is 97° and the measure of angle 7 is 83°, are ℓ1 and ℓ2 parallel?

6. If ℓ1 and ℓ2 are parallel and the measure of angle 4 is 65°, what is the measure of angle 6?

7. If the measure of angle 6 is 109° and the measure of angle 7 is 73°, are ℓ1 and ℓ2 parallel?

8. If ℓ1 and ℓ2 are parallel and the measure of angle 1 is 90°, what are the measures of every other angle?

Solutions – Lines and Angles

1. If the measure of angle 2 is 77°, what is the measure of angle 5?

77°

2. If the measure of angle 2 is 77°, what is the measure of angle 1?

103°

3. What is the sum of the measures of angles 1, 2, 5, and 6?

360°

4. If $\ell1$ and $\ell2$ are parallel and the measure of angle 8 is 104°, what is the measure of angle 6?

104°

5. If the measure of angle 1 is 97° and the measure of angle 7 is 83°, are $\ell1$ and $\ell2$ parallel?

Yes

6. If $\ell1$ and $\ell2$ are parallel and the measure of angle 4 is 65°, what is the measure of angle 6?

115°

7. If the measure of angle 6 is 109° and the measure of angle 7 is 73°, are $\ell1$ and $\ell2$ parallel?

No

8. If $\ell1$ and $\ell2$ are parallel and the measure of angle 1 is 90°, what are the measures of every other angle?

90°

Triangles

The **sum** of the angles in a triangle is always **180°**, regardless of shape.

If you know **two angles** of a triangle you can always find the third angle:

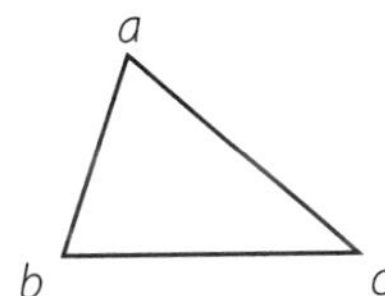

We know $a + b + c = 180$.

If we are told that a is 70° and c is 50° then we can find b by substituting the variables we know with their values

$$70 + b + 50 = 180 \;\rightarrow\; b = 180 - 70 - 50 \;\rightarrow\; b = 60°$$

The **perimeter** of a triangle is the sum of the length of its sides. $\quad P = a + b + c$

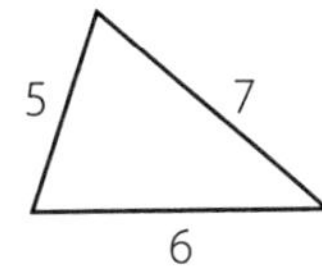

Perimeter: $5 + 6 + 7 = 18$

GMAT Insider: Triangles are the most important geometric shape on the GMAT. We will go into depth on triangles in the Geometry lesson.

The **area** of a triangle is its base multiplied by its height divided by 2.

$$A = \frac{b \cdot h}{2}$$

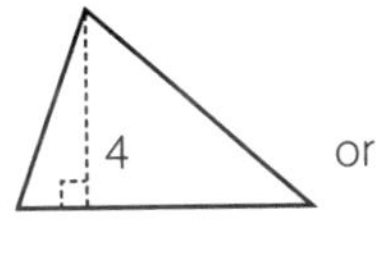 or 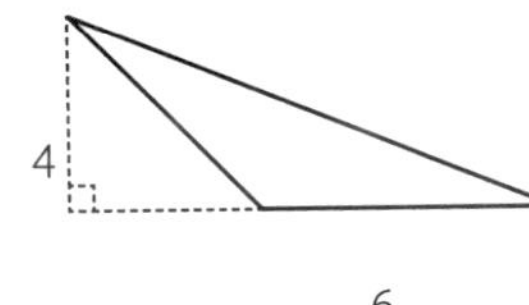

Area: $A = \frac{6 \cdot 4}{2} = 12$

The **height** or **altitude** of a triangle is defined as the distance from the base to the opposing apex. The altitude is always perpendicular to the base.

Any side can be the base, and the area is the same for **all** base/height combinations in the same triangle. The **longest side** of a triangle is always the side **opposite the greatest angle**. The **shortest** side of a triangle is always the side **opposite the smallest angle**.

Triangles Drill

1. In triangle ABC, if angle A measures 37° and angle B measures 55°, what is the measure of angle C?

2. What is the perimeter of a triangle with sides of 4, 5, and 7?

3. If the perimeter of triangle DEF is 17, and two of the sides measure 3 and 8, what is the length of the third side?

4. If a triangle has a base of 5 and a height (perpendicular to the base) of 4, what is the area of the triangle?

5. If triangle ABC has an area of 12, and the height perpendicular to one of the sides has a length of 4, what is the length of that side?

6. If a triangle has sides of length 2, 3, and 4, and the height perpendicular to the side with length 2 is 3, what is the perimeter and area of the triangle?

7. If a triangle has an area of $4\sqrt{3}$, a perimeter of 12, and all 3 sides are of equal length, what is the height of the triangle?

8. If the perimeter of triangle XYZ is 12, one side is 5, another side is 4, and the height perpendicular to the third side is 3, what is the triangle's area?

Solutions – Triangles

1. In triangle ABC, if angle A measures 37° and angle B measures 55°, what is the measure of angle C?

88°

2. What is the perimeter of a triangle with sides of 4, 5, and 7?

16

3. If the perimeter of triangle DEF is 17, and two of the sides measure 3 and 8, what is the length of the third side?

6

4. If a triangle has a base of 5 and a height (perpendicular to the base) of 4, what is the area of the triangle?

10

5. If triangle ABC has an area of 12, and the height perpendicular to one of the sides has a length of 4, what is the length of that side?

6

6. If a triangle has sides of length 2, 3, and 4, and the height perpendicular to the side with length 2 is 3, what is the perimeter and area of the triangle?

perimeter = 9; area = 3

7. If a triangle has an area of $4\sqrt{3}$, a perimeter of 12, and all 3 sides are of equal length, what is the height of the triangle?

$2\sqrt{3}$

8. If the perimeter of triangle XYZ is 12, one side is 5, another side is 4, and the height perpendicular to the third side is 3, what is the triangle's area?

4.5

Quadrilaterals

Quadrilateral literally means "four-sided". The angles in a quadrilateral always add up to 360°. The four most frequently encountered types of quadrilaterals on the GMAT are:

I.) **Square**

GMAT Insider: As with equilateral triangles, when you know one measurement of a square you know them all (including side, area, and perimeter).

a. Every side is the same length and opposite sides are parallel.

b. Every angle is 90°.

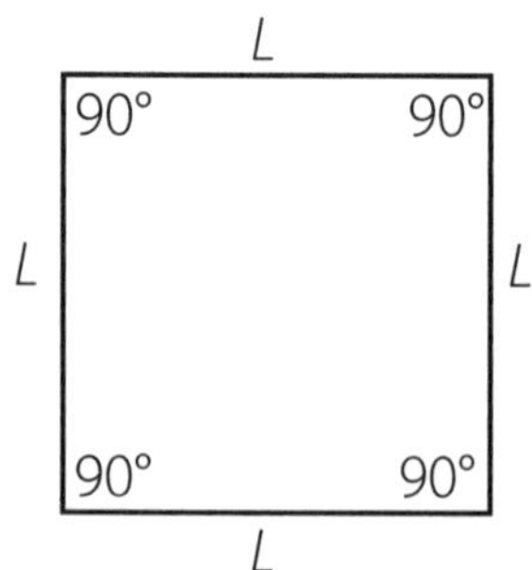

Facts & Formulas: That the lengths of all the sides are the same does not necessarily mean the figure is a square. If the angles are not 90°, the figure is called a **rhombus**.

Area: L^2 **Perimeter:** $4L$

II.) **Rectangle**

a. Opposite sides are parallel and of the same length.

b. Every angle is 90°.

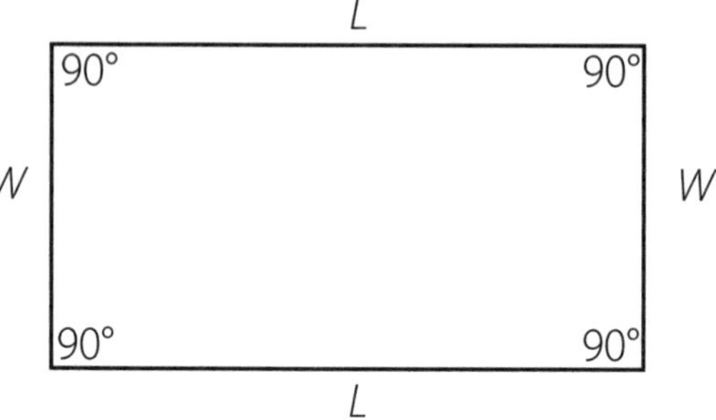

Area: $L \cdot W$ **Perimeter:** $2L + 2W$

III.)   Parallelogram

    a.   Opposite sides are parallel and of the same length

    b.   The interior angles add up to 360°

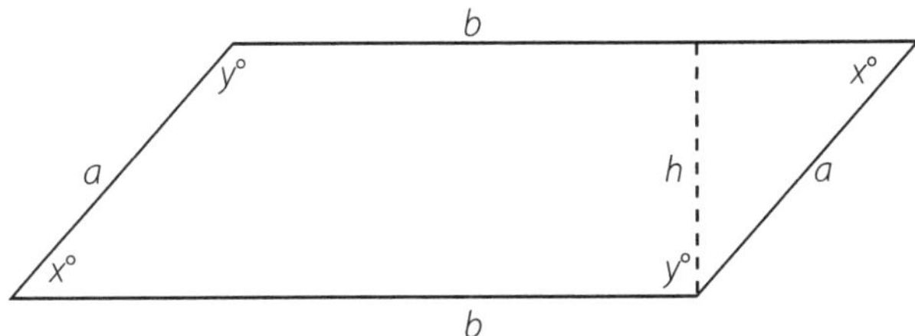

h = height

Area: $b \cdot h$ **Perimeter:** $2a + 2b$

IV.)   Trapezoid

    a.   Two sides are parallel

    b.   The interior angles add up to 360°

> *Facts & Formulas:* For any of the quadrilaterals, the area is equal to the base multiplied by the height— but remember that the height must form a right angle with the base, and the base must be one value. Hence, trapezoids' bases must be averaged, and parallelograms and trapezoids will require you to create perpendicular height.

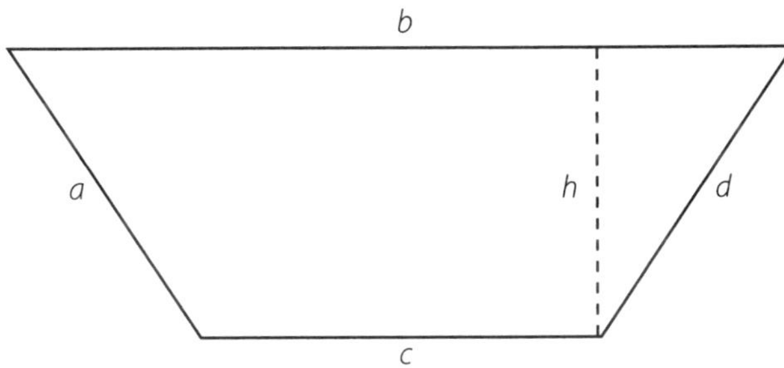

Area: $\frac{1}{2}(b + c) \cdot h$ **Perimeter:** $a + b + c + d$

Because you can't use either b or c as the base, we find the average of the two when calculating the area of a trapezoid.

Quadrilaterals Drill

1. What is the area of a square with perimeter 20?

2. What is the width of a rectangle with area 15 and length 5?

3. If a parallelogram has area 30, perimeter 26, and two of the sides have length 6, what is the length of each of the other two sides?

4. If a trapezoid has area 24, height 6, and one of the parallel sides has length 3, what is the length of the other parallel side?

5. If a quadrilateral has four 90° angles and sides of length 3, 3, 8, and 8, it is which of the following figures: square, rectangle, parallelogram, trapezoid?

6. If three angles of a quadrilateral have measures 35°, 145°, and 35°, is it a parallelogram?

7. If all of a quadrilateral's sides have length 2, is it a square?

8. If all of a quadrilateral's sides have length 2 and its area is 4, is it a square?

Solutions – Quadrilaterals

1. What is the area of a square with perimeter 20?

25

2. What is the width of a rectangle with area 15 and length 5?

3

3. If a parallelogram has area 30, perimeter 26, and two of the sides have length 6, what is the length of each of the other two sides?

7

4. If a trapezoid has area 24, height 6, and one of the parallel sides has length 3, what is the length of the other parallel side?

5

5. If a quadrilateral has four 90° angles and sides of length 3, 3, 8, and 8, it is which of the following figures: square, rectangle, parallelogram, trapezoid?

Rectangle, parallelogram, and trapezoid, but not square

6. If three angles of a quadrilateral have measures 35°, 145°, and 35°, is it a parallelogram?

Not necessarily (the two 35° angles aren't necessarily opposite eachother – the figure might be a trapezoid).

7. If all of a quadrilateral's sides have length 2, is it a square?

Not necessarily (it could be a rhombus)

8. If all of a quadrilateral's sides have length 2 and its area is 4, is it a square?

Yes.

Circles

As in arithmetic, it is essential that students are confident with their definitions in geometry. Let's discuss important circle definitions:

1. Radius

The **radius** of a circle describes the distance from the center of a circle to the circle itself.

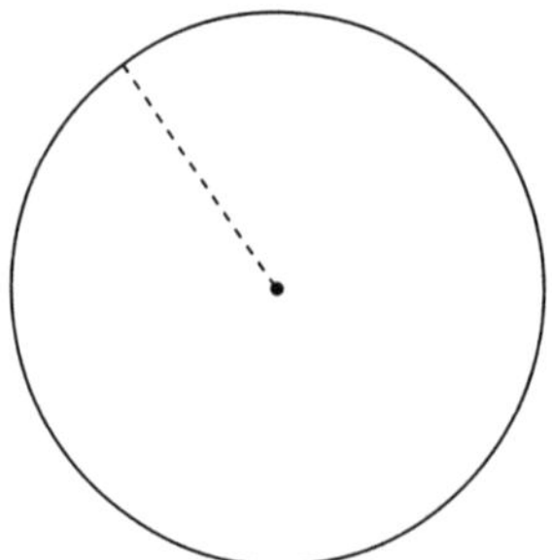

2. Diameter

The **diameter** of a circle describes the distance from one side of the circle to the other side, intersecting the center of the circle. **The diameter is twice the length of the radius.**

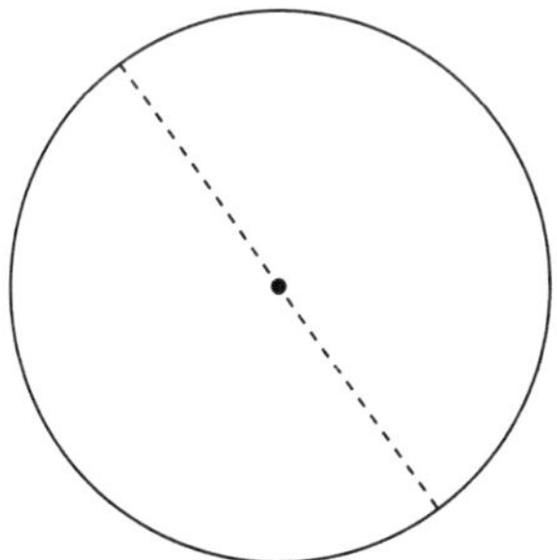

3. Chord

A line that connects any two points on a circle is known as a chord. The diameter of a circle is an example of a chord.

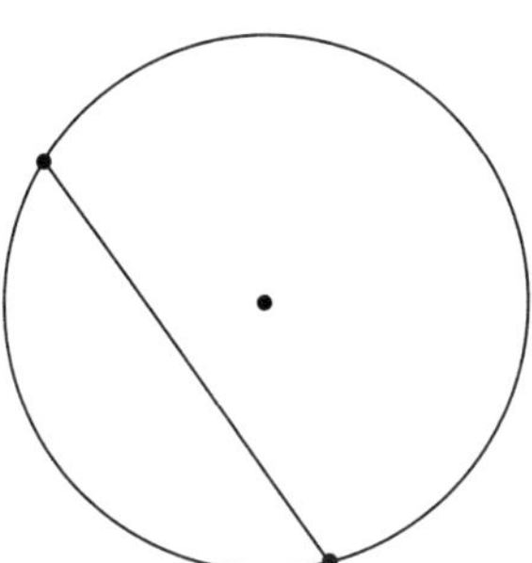

Circle Formulas

π (pronounced pie, spelled "pi") is a symbol that describes a number that is essential when solving mathematical problems involving circles. π is the ratio of the circumference of a circle to the diameter of that circle. The circumference is the distance around a circle (eqivalent to the perimeter of a polygon). $\pi = 3.14$*. Since fractions often simplify arithmetic on the GMAT, knowing that π can also be expressed as $\frac{22}{7}$ may be helpful.

GMAT Insider: Many geometry problems start with your knowledge of particular geometry rules and formulas. Once you have applied those rules, most of the problems turn into algebra problems as seen in this example.

1. Area: πr^2 (where r = radius)

2. Circumference: $2\pi r$ **or** πd (where d = diameter)

Example: If the circumference of a circle is x, then express the area of that circle in terms of x.

If $2\pi r = x$ then we can express r in terms of x. $r = \frac{x}{2\pi}$. With one more substitution we can see that $A = \pi\left(\frac{x}{2\pi}\right)^2$ Simplifying further, we see that $A = \frac{\pi x^2}{4\pi^2}$ By cancelling the π from the top and the bottom the final answer is $A = \frac{x^2}{4\pi}$.

* π is an irrational number as it has an infinite number of decimal places. However, for the purposes of the GMAT, it is sufficient to know the first two decimal places.

Circles Drill

1. If a circle has a radius of 2, what is its area?

2. If a circle has a circumference of 24π, what is its area?

3. If a circle has an area of 81π, what is the length of the circle's longest chord?

4. Circle A has a radius of 7 and Circle B has a circumference of 15π. Which is the larger circle?

5. If a circular pizza pie with a diameter of 16 inches is cut into eighths, what is the area of each of the slices?

6. If a circle has an area of 9π, which of the following could be the lengths of chords on that circle: 1, 3, 4, 6, 7, 8?

7. If a car's tires cover 20π inches for every revolution, what is the outer diameter of each of the tires?

8. If 20 circular pepperoni slices each with a 1-inch diameter cover a circular pizza pie with diameter 14 inches, what fraction of the pizza is covered with pepperoni slices?

Solutions – Circles

1. If a circle has a radius of 2, what is its area?

4π

2. If a circle has a circumference of 24π, what is its area?

144π

3. If a circle has an area of 81π, what is the length of the circle's longest chord?

18

4. Circle A has a radius of 7 and Circle B has a circumference of 15π. Which is the larger circle?

Circle B

5. If a circular pizza pie with a diameter of 16 inches is cut into eighths, what is the area of each of the slices?

8π square inches

6. If a circle has an area of 9π, which of the following could be the lengths of chords on that circle: 1, 3, 4, 6, 7, 8?

1, 3, 4, and 6 only

7. If a car's tires cover 20π inches for every revolution, what is the outer diameter of each of the tires?

20 inches

8. If 20 circular pepperoni slices each with a 1-inch diameter cover a circular pizza pie with diameter 14 inches, what fraction of the pizza is covered with pepperoni slices?

$\dfrac{5}{49}$

Coordinate Geometry

Coordinate geometry is an area of increasing importance on the GMAT. Students are reporting that they have faced multiple questions on coordinate geometry on their tests. Let's go over the basic definitions and properties of the coordinate geometry plane:

The following figure is called a **coordinate plane.**

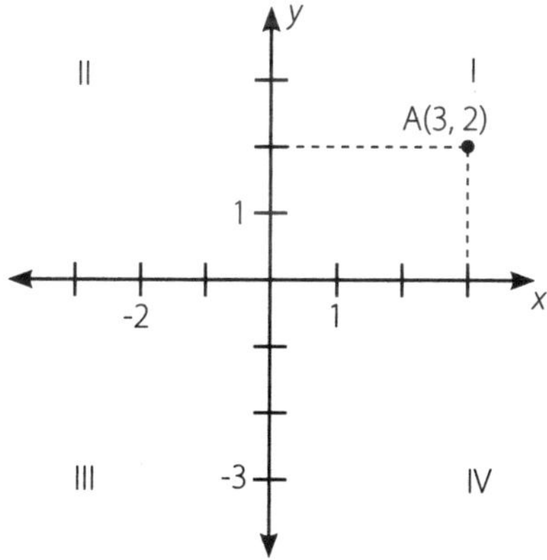

Definitions for the Coordinate Geometry Plane:

1. The coordinate geometry plane has 4 distinct quadrants that are labeled above and go from I to IV in a counterclockwise direction.

2. The horizontal line is the **x-axis**.

3. The vertical line is the **y-axis**.

4. The intersection of the x-axis and y-axis is the **origin**.

5. Every point on the coordinate plane can be described by an **ordered pair (x, y)**, where x describes where the point is on the x-axis and y describes where the point is on the y-axis. The signs of x and y determine which quandrant the point will lie in.

Lines in the Coordinate Geometry Plane:

All algebraic equations that are linear (have no exponents greater than 1) can be mapped on the coordinate geometry plane as a straight line. It is easiest to map that line on the coordinate geometry plane when the equation is in the following form:

$y = mx + b$

1. Slope

In the equation $y = mx + b$, m describes the slope of the line.

The higher m is, the steeper the line. This can be seen by setting $b = 0$ and trying different values for m. If $m = 1, 2,$ or, 3, then we have equations $y = x$, $y = 2x$, and $y = 3x$, respectively. When $x = 0$, $y = 0$ in all of these equations. But when $x = 1$, the equations with the bigger slope (the higher values of m) will have higher values for y, as seen in the diagram at right. The slope of a line can be found by:

$$\frac{\text{change in } y \text{ coordinate}}{\text{change in } x \text{ coordinate}} = \frac{y_2 - y_1}{x_2 - x_1} = \text{slope}$$

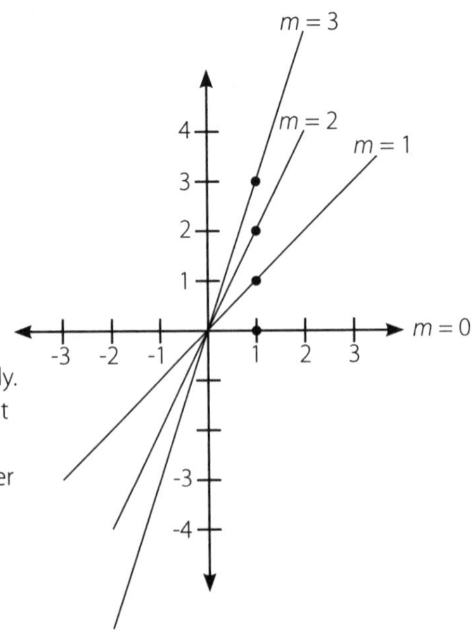

If the slope has a positive value, the line will be pointing up to the right.
If the slope has a negative value, the line will be pointing down to the right.

What is the slope of the line in this diagram?

$$\frac{\text{change in } y \text{ coordinate}}{\text{change in } x \text{ coordinate}} = \text{slope}$$

$$\frac{10 - (-20)}{20 - (-40)} = \frac{30}{60} = \frac{1}{2} = 0.5$$

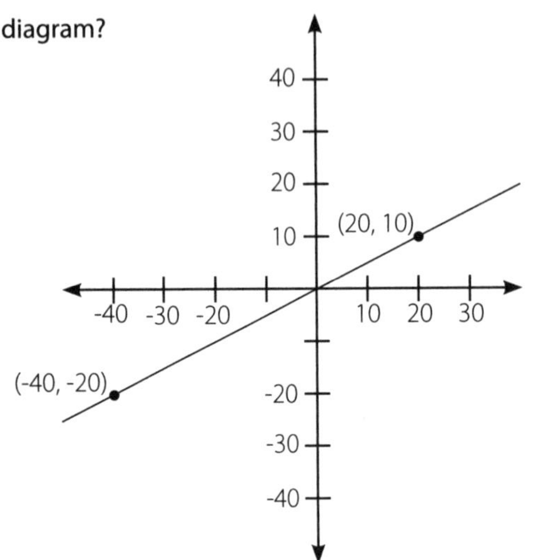

2. *x* and *y* intercepts

In the equation $y = mx + b$, b describes the intersection with the *y*-axis, known as the **y-intercept.**

The higher *b* is, the higher up the line intersects the *y*-axis. Again, this can be seen by setting $m = 1$ and $x = 0$, and trying different values for *b*.

The point where the line intersects the *x*-axis is called the **x-intercept**. The *x*-intercept can be found by setting $y = 0$.

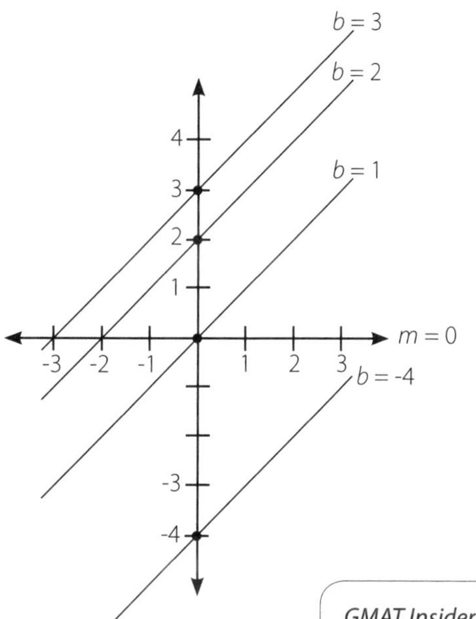

The equation $y = mx + b$ descibes a straight line with the following properties:

$$y\text{-intercept} = b \qquad x\text{-intercept} = -\frac{b}{m} \qquad slope = m$$

GMAT Insider: The ability to quickly find *x* and *y* intercepts is one of the most important skills for coordinate geometry.

Coordinate Geometry Drill

1. What is the slope of the line connecting points (2, 4) and (8, 2)?

2. What is the y-intercept of the line formed by the equation $y = 4x + 3$?

3. What is the x-intercept of the line formed by the equation $y = 6x - 2$?

4. If the x-intercept of a line is 3 and the y-intercept is 4, what is the equation of the line?

5. Does the point (2, 3) lie on the line formed by the equation $y = 2x + 3$?

6. If a line intercepts the y-axis at $y = 4$ and has a slope of 2, at what value of x will it cross the x-axis?

7. What is the slope of $y = 4$?

8. If a line is described by the equation $y = 3x-1$, what is the x-coordinate of the point on the line at which $y = 4$?

Solutions – Coordinate Geometry

1. What is the slope of the line connecting points (2, 4) and (8, 2)?

$-\dfrac{1}{3}$

2. What is the y-intercept of the line formed by the equation $y = 4x + 3$?

3

3. What is the x-intercept of the line formed by the equation $y = 6x - 2$?

$\dfrac{1}{3}$

4. If the x-intercept of a line is 3 and the y-intercept is 4, what is the equation of the line?

$y = -\dfrac{4x}{3} + 4$

5. Does the point (2, 3) lie on the line formed by the equation $y = 2x + 3$?

No

6. If a line intercepts the y-axis at $y = 4$ and has a slope of 2, at what value of x will it cross the x-axis?

-2

7. What is the slope of $y = 4$?

0

8. If a line is described by the equation $y = 3x-1$, what is the x-coordinate of the point on the line at which $y = 4$?

$\dfrac{5}{3}$

THE MBA TOUR

Your future begins here

The MBA Tour offers Quality Interaction With Top Business Schools

MEET with school representatives at our OPEN FAIR

LISTEN to top school experts discuss valuable MBA admission topics at our PANEL PRESENTATIONS

DISCUSS individual school qualities with representatives at our ROUNDTABLE EVENTS

ASIA	UNITED STATES	SOUTH AMERICA	CANADA
TOKYO	HOUSTON	BUENOS AIRES	CALGARY
SEOUL	CHICAGO	SANTIAGO	VANCOUVER
TAIPEI	ATLANTA	SAO PAULO	TORONTO
BEIJING	NEW YORK	LIMA	MONTREAL
SHANGHAI	BOSTON	BOGOTA	
BANGKOK	WASHINGTON DC	MEXICO CITY	
SINGAPORE	LOS ANGELES		
	SAN FRANCISCO	EUROPE	
INDIA		MUNICH	
BANGALORE		LONDON	
NEW DELHI		PARIS	
MUMBAI			

Register at **www.thembatour.com**

THE MBA TOUR
Your future begins here